MW01010140

Fw 190 Defence of the Reich Aces

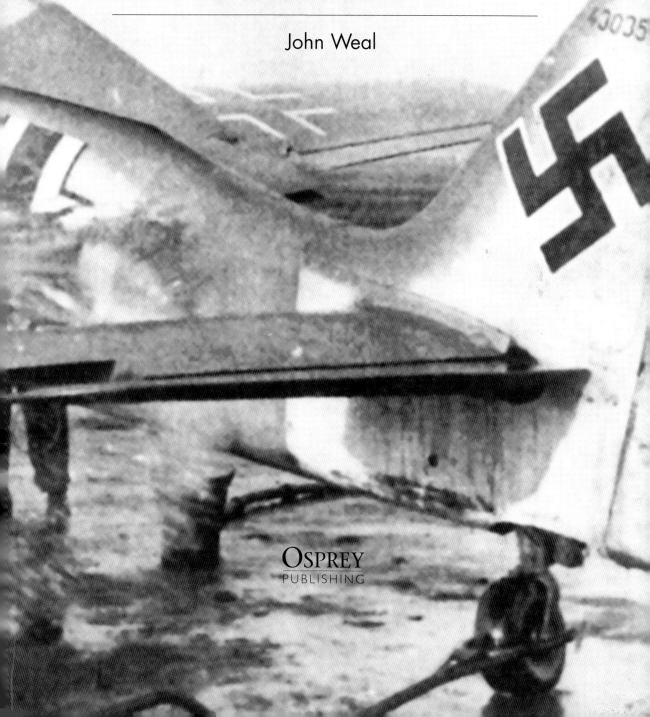

SERIES EDITOR: TONY HOLMES

OSPREY AIRCRAFT OF THE ACES • 92

Fw 190 Defence of the Reich Aces

John Weal

OSPREY
PUBLISHING

Front Cover

For four long years from the fall of France in the summer of 1940 until D-Day, 6 June 1944, two of the Luftwaffe's most famous *Jagdgeschwader* – JG 2 'Richthofen' and JG 26 'Schlageter' – guarded the airspace of northwestern Europe against the growing might of Allied air power. They also constituted the first line of defence against the US Army Air Force's daylight bombing offensive against western Germany. By the end of the war both *Geschwader* had been incorporated into the Defence of the Reich organisation proper.

Although they did not rack up the astronomical numbers of kills claimed by Luftwaffe fighter pilots on the eastern front, many members of JGs 2 and 26 achieved considerable success against the Western Allies. A stellar trio, Adolf Galland, Egon Mayer and 'Pips' Priller, topped the century mark, while many more either exceeded or approached their half-centuries. Among the latter was Knight's Cross holder Oberleutnant Gerhard Vogt of II./JG 26. Having first joined the *Gruppe* as an Obergefreiter in 1941, Vogt's eventual tally of 48 western victories included eight USAAF heavy bombers.

Mark Postlethwaite's striking cover painting reconstructs Gerhard Vogt's final mission. On the morning of 14 January 1945, II./JG 26's four *Staffeln* of Fw 190D-9 'Long-noses' took off from a foggy Nordhorn to attack American fighter-bombers reported active in the St Vith area of Belgium. However, their route south put them on a collision course with a large formation of Flying Fortresses heading for the Rhine road bridges at Cologne. Alerted to the presence of the Luftwaffe force, some two-dozen P-51 Mustangs of the 78th Fighter Group were detached from the B-17s' fighter escort and ordered to engage the Focke-Wulfs. They bounced the lower-flying Germans near Aachen, and one of the pilots lost in the ensuing action was the *Staffelkapitän* of 5./JG 26, Oberleutnant Gerhard Vogt. His 'White 13' was last seen disappearing into cloud to the southeast of Cologne

First published in Great Britain in 2011 by Osprey Publishing
Midland House, West Way, Botley, Oxford, OX2 0PH, UK
44-02 23rd St, Suite 219, Long Island City, NY 11101, USA

E-mail: info@ospreypublishing.com

© 2011 Osprey Publishing Limited

ISBN 13; 978 1 84603 482 4
E-book ISBN: 9 781 84908 294 5

Edited by Tony Holmes
Page design by Tony Truscott
Cover Artwork by Mark Postlethwaite
Aircraft Profiles by John Weal
Index by Alan Thatcher
Originated by PDQ Digital Media Solutions
Printed and bound in China through Bookbuilders

11 12 13 14 15   10 9 8 7 6 5 4 3 2 1

Osprey Publishing is supporting the Woodland Trust, the UK's leading woodland conservation charity by funding the dedication of trees.

www.ospreypublishing.com

CONTENTS

GUARDIANS OF THE NORTHERN SHORES

When the famous American aviator Colonel Charles Lindbergh, the first man to fly solo across the Atlantic, visited Berlin in July 1936 he was welcomed at Staaken airfield by Oberst Kastner on behalf of Luftwaffe C-in-C Hermann Göring, and by Herr Wolfgang von Gronau, President of the German Aero Club. Lindbergh was hugely impressed by what he saw on his conducted tours of some of the Third Reich's leading military and sports aviation facilities. At one luncheon given in his honour at Döberitz he was moved to propose a toast. 'To the bombers – may they always be slower. To the pursuit machines – may they always be faster!'

Lindbergh's words were greeted by a roar of approval from his hosts for Döberitz was home to Major Carl Vieck's I./JG 132 'Richthofen', and his table companions flew Germany's then fastest 'pursuit machine', the Heinkel He 51 fighter.

While the ill-judged toast was no doubt music to the ears of Major Vieck and the pilots of his three *Staffeln*, it is unlikely that many more than a handful of the countless thousands of American boys currently enjoying their school vacations in this summer of 1936 were even aware of the sentiments being expressed by their illustrious compatriot in far-off Germany. It was perhaps just as well, for in little more than six years' time many of those selfsame schoolboys would be manning the bombers of the American Eighth Air Force high in the skies above Hitler's Third Reich, trying desperately to squeeze the last ounce of power and speed out of their B-17 Flying Fortresses and B-24 Liberators as they sought to escape from the deadly attentions of the Luftwaffe's fighters.

The first daylight bombing raids on Germany had been launched within hours of Britain declaring war on 3 September 1939. However, the Royal Air Force's twin-engined bombers proved totally inadequate for the task. After a series of horrendous losses, the British had been forced to restrict their air offensive against the Third Reich almost exclusively to the hours of darkness. Following the disastrous 'Battle of the German Bight' on 18 December 1939, when 17 out of a force of 22 Wellingtons sent to attack Wilhelmshaven were either lost or written-off, three years of relative aerial calm had settled along Germany's North Sea shores.

Throughout this period the northern sector served partly as a 'nursery slope' for newly activated *Jagdgruppen* needing to acclimatise themselves to operational service, and partly as a rest and recuperation area for established *Gruppen* on their way either from or to other more active fronts. For the first two of those three years very little happened as an ever-changing miscellany of different *Gruppen* and individual *Staffeln* guarded the North Sea frontier against an enemy rendered conspicuous only by his absence.

From small acorns. The Eighth Air Force's first mission was undertaken on 4 July 1942 by six US-crewed RAF Boston light bombers. Two failed to return. The aircraft seen here is not one of that unfortunate pair, however, but a similar machine (of No 88 Sqn RAF) brought down by Hauptmann Johannes Naumann, *Staffelkapitän* of 6./JG 26, over a year later on 26 July 1943, by which time the budding Defence of the Reich ace – seen here sitting atop his prize – already had two American Flying Fortresses to his name

Then, on 11 December 1941, exactly one week short of the second anniversary of the 'Battle of the German Bight', and following hard on the heels of the Japanese attack on Pearl Harbor, Hitler declared war on America. Suddenly the future looked very different. The Führer's announcement heralded the inevitable appearance of a new opponent on the European scene, and one, moreover, who held totally different views on strategic bombing from those of the RAF, whose Bomber Command was by this time fully and irrevocably committed to pursuing its night offensive.

The Americans were firm believers in daylight precision bombing, and they were to lose as little time as possible in putting those beliefs into practice. The first aircrews of the embryonic Eighth Air Force arrived in the United Kingdom on 11 May 1942, five months to the day since Hitler's declaration of war. They immediately began training with an RAF squadron that was equipped with Douglas Boston light bombers.

Symbolically, the Eighth Air Force's first operation was flown on American Independence Day, 4 July 1942. It was a combined Anglo-American mission with 12 RAF Bostons – six crewed by Americans – being despatched to bomb Luftwaffe airfields in Holland. Three of the Bostons failed to return. One, flown by an RAF crew, fell victim to a Luftwaffe fighter, while the other two, crewed by the USAAF, were both shot down by flak. They were to be the American squadron's only combat losses as part of the Eighth Air Force. After two more operations flown under their own colours (albeit in ex-RAF machines), the 15th Bomb Squadron (Light) was transferred to the Mediterranean theatre in September to join the USAAF's Twelfth Air Force.

Even before the Bostons' Independence Day mission, the first of the Eight Air Force's four-engined 'heavies' – the B-17 Flying Fortresses of the 97th Bomb Group (BG) – had already touched down in England.

Twelve of their number then flew the Eighth Air Force's first heavy bomber raid on 17 August 1942. The target was the marshalling yard at Rouen/Sotteville, in northern France. All the aircraft got back safely, although two bore evidence of slight flak damage.

A further three weeks would pass before the first European B-17 combat loss occurred. This dubious honour fell to the 97th BG's B-17F 41-24445 *Southern Belle*, which was part of a mixed force of some 50 Flying Fortresses sent to bomb the French Potez aircraft factory at Méaulte, east of Amiens, on 6 September. It was brought down by the Fw 190 flown by Hauptmann Karl-Heinz 'Conny' Meyer, the *Gruppenkommandeur* of II./JG 26. Little more than ten minutes after Meyer's victim had crash-landed northwest of Amiens, one of his pilots, Oberfeldwebel Willi Roth of 4. *Staffel*, was credited with another of the Flying Fortresses. 41-9026 *Baby Doll*, a B-17E of the 92nd BG, made it back as far as the coast before going down into the Channel about four miles off Le Tréport.

This was just the beginning of a long and bloody conflict for both attackers and defenders alike. Although the Americans' intentions were already clear, for the moment they were content to cut their operational teeth on cross-Channel and short-range missions against targets situated in the coastal regions of northern and western France and the Low Countries. Then, as their numbers and confidence grew, they would begin to push deeper into northwest Europe. It could only be a matter of time before they entered German airspace and started to attack targets within the Reich itself.

The Luftwaffe High Command was under no illusions. It knew that the American heavy bombers were coming. Two of the Luftwaffe's most experienced *Jagdgeschwader*, JGs 2 and 26, had long been stationed in northwest Europe as the first line of defence against daylight incursions by RAF fighters and light bombers. So important was their role deemed to be that by the summer of 1942 both these units had been almost entirely equipped with the most advanced fighter in the Luftwaffe's armoury, the Focke-Wulf Fw 190.

Although not part of the Defence of the Reich organisation proper in the early years, the two western-based *Jagdgeschwader*, JGs 2 and 26, often provided the first line of defence against incursions by US heavy bombers. A mechanic quickly scrambles out of the way as the pilot of 7./JG 2's 'White 9' guns his engine

But what of Germany's own North Sea coastal belt? The launch of a daylight strategic bombing offensive by the Eighth Air Force against the Reich would automatically transform this hitherto relatively thinly defended backwater into one of the main aerial approach routes into the heart of Hitler's empire. What was being done to strengthen this potentially vital sector?

In fact, the first moves towards this end had been made as far back as the winter of 1940-41, when three hitherto completely separate *Jagdstaffeln* deployed across northwest Germany had been amalgamated to form a new *Jagdgruppe*, I./JG 1. There *had* been an earlier I./JG 1 dating back to before the war, but this unit had been redesignated to become III./JG 27 at the start of the Battle of Britain.

It would be almost another nine months before a II./JG 1 was added to the Luftwaffe's order of battle. Unlike I./JG 1, however, this new formation was created not from scratch, but by the simple process of redesignating an already existing *Jagdgruppe*. The experienced I./JG 3, which was a veteran of the Battles of France and Britain, had just returned to Germany after participating in the opening rounds of Operation *Barbarossa*, the invasion of the Soviet Union. In the early weeks of 1942 two further *Gruppen* were brought into being. III. and IV./JG 1 were both made up out of *Ergänzungs* and *Einsatzstaffeln* from other *Jagdgeschwader* (specifically, from JGs 2, 27, 52 and 2, 26, 51, respectively).

After being transferred up into Denmark and southern Norway in February, the first short-lived IV./JG 1 was incorporated into the embryonic JG 5, however, and a replacement IV./JG 1 had to be put together during March and April 1942 using intakes from various fighter training schools.

Despite the decidedly heterogeneous nature of its background, JG 1 was quickly slotted into position along the right-hand flank of the unbroken chain of Luftwaffe day fighter defences of northwest Europe that now stretched from the Bay of Biscay to the Kattegat. By the late summer of 1942, when the Eighth Air Force was beginning to make its first exploratory forays into northern France, three of the *Geschwader's* four component *Gruppen* had also been re-equipped with the Fw 190 to bring it up almost on a par with neighbouring JGs 2 and 26.

By January 1943 the stage was thus set, and one cast of players had already taken their places. Guarding the all-important German Bight sector, JG 1's four *Gruppen* were deployed in an arc from southern Norway down into the Netherlands as they awaited the first attack on their homeland by American heavy bombers. That attack was to be delivered on 27 January 1943.

Despite all the time, effort and resources each side had put into preparing for this moment, the Eighth Air Force's raid on Wilhelmshaven – the opening blow to be struck in the daylight Defence of the Reich campaign – proved somewhat inconclusive. This did not prevent both protagonists from publicly claiming it as a victory, however. The northern German port of Wilhelmshaven had also been the target for the RAF on 18 December 1939, and like the 22 Wellingtons that had carried out that raid just over three years before, the 64 B-17s despatched against the port on 27 January 1943 went in unescorted.

There, the similarity between the two missions ended. The Americans were not cut to pieces in a second great 'Battle of the German Bight'. In

fact, they were intercepted by just one *Gruppe* – the Bf 109s of I./JG 1 stationed at Jever, some eight miles outside Wilhelmshaven. The Flying Fortresses lived up to their name, for their defensive firepower, combined with the Bf 109 pilots' inexperience in tackling these new adversaries, kept their losses to a minimum. Although I./JG 1 somewhat optimistically claimed five B-17s destroyed, only one bomber was actually shot down.

Meanwhile, a smaller force of 27 B-24 Liberators approaching Wilhelmshaven on a more southerly route had failed to find the target altogether due to 'bad weather and poor navigation'. This formation then fell foul of elements of the two Fw 190-equipped *Gruppen* of JG 1 based in Holland, II. and IV./JG 1. Two of the Liberators, both from the 44th BG, went down into the shallows between the Dutch coast and the offshore island of Terschelling. One source suggests that the first bomber was lost as the result of a mid-air collision with an already battle-damaged Fw 190, which tore off the B-24's port wing and tail assembly.

While far from certain, if this *is* the case it means that the first victory claimed by an Fw 190 in Defence of the Reich was achieved by Feldwebel Fritz Koch of 12./JG 1. It would also make it Koch's only known success, and one he did not survive to celebrate, for he too went down into the mud of the Waddenzee, off Terschelling, in the wreckage of his 'Yellow 3'. Nor is it possible to state with absolute certainty which of the four pilots of II. and IV./JG 1 officially credited with the destruction of a Liberator on this date (the four names do not include that of Fritz Koch, incidentally) was responsible for downing the second B-24.

Although JG 1 had claimed nine heavy bombers shot down, the Americans had, in fact, lost just three aircraft. On the other side of the coin, the bombers' gunners submitted claims for a total of 22 Luftwaffe fighters destroyed, a further 14 probably destroyed and 13 others damaged. JG 1 actually lost seven aircraft (five Bf 109s and two Fw 190s), with three pilots killed and one wounded. Such overclaiming was understandable, indeed almost inevitable, given the unique nature of fighter-versus-bomber combat – the tautened nerves, the savagery of the initial assault, the heat

Things did not always go smoothly. 'White 2' of 7./JG 26 was involved in a taxiing accident at Wevelghem in August 1942. After repair, this machine later went to JG 51 in the USSR, where it crashed near Smolensk early in 1943

and confusion of battle, the intensity of individual split-second actions and the fragmentary images and impressions these left in the mind.

Exaggerated claims were very rarely the result of deliberate falsification. Anyone suspected of such behaviour would receive very short shrift from his fellow pilots. The most common reason for the inflated totals was that all too often there would be multiple claimants for the same victory, each convinced in his own mind – and in all good faith – that he alone was responsible for his opponent's demise. Despite strict checks introduced by both sides, the problem was never satisfactorily resolved. It was to remain a constant throughout the 27 months of the Defence of the Reich campaign and, if anything, worsened as the numbers of aircraft involved in the ferocious air battles in the skies over Germany grew from dozens into the hundreds and finally to thousands.

Returning to the early days, the Eighth Air Force's second attempted foray into Reich airspace – to the marshalling yards at Hamm on 2 February – was thwarted not by JG 1, but by the bad weather over the North Sea that forced all six bomber groups to turn back. Forty-eight hours later they tried again, but once more Hamm was saved by the adverse weather. The Eighth's two B-24 groups aborted before reaching the Dutch coast, but most of the B-17s ploughed on to unload their bombs on the German North Sea port of Emden instead.

The Flying Fortresses were intercepted by elements of the same three *Gruppen* of JG 1 that they had encountered during the Wilhelmshaven raid eight days earlier (reinforced on this occasion by a number of Bf 110 nightfighters operating temporarily by day). The Bf 109s of I./JG 1 again claimed a single B-17, this time without loss to themselves. The Fw 190s accounted for five Flying Fortresses destroyed, but it cost them three pilots killed. II./JG 1 suffered mixed fortunes. While Hauptmann Dietrich Wickop, the *Staffelkapitän* of 5./JG 1, was apparently credited with the first B-17 to be lost – a lone bomber he sent down into the Waddenzee east of Den Helder – fellow *Staffelkapitän* Oberleutnant Walter Leonhardt of 6./JG 1 was shot down in flames attacking a sizeable formation of Flying Fortresses out over the North Sea. Although he was seen to take to his parachute, Leonhardt was never found.

The two other Fw 190 pilots lost were both members of IV./JG 1. One of them, 12. *Staffel's* Unteroffizier Rudolf Mayer, was also involved in a mid-air collision (with a B-17 to the southeast of Emden). As with Feldwebel Koch of the same *Staffel*, who had collided with the B-24 on 27 January, Mayer was not officially credited with the bomber that he had destroyed. JG 1's claims for six bombers downed tallies reasonably well with the five B-17s actually lost, but only if one ignores the three Flying Fortresses credited to the Bf 110s of IV./NJG 1 in this action!

The weather was again the saviour of Hamm on 14 February, forcing the four groups of B-17s sent to attack the marshalling yards on that date to turn back after crossing the Dutch coast. It would be another 12 days before the Eighth's next incursion into Reich airspace, and again the maximum effort directed by all six groups against Bremen on 26 February also fell foul of bad weather. With Bremen obscured by cloud, the force turned to Wilhelmshaven as a target of opportunity. That decision cost them seven of their number – five B-17s and two B-24s, which was the highest number of losses suffered by USAAF 'heavies' in a single day to date.

The one-eyed Günther Specht was one of the leading personalities of the Defence of the Reich campaign, but the great majority of his 15 reported heavy bomber victories were achieved while flying Bf 109s with JG 11. He is pictured here wearing the German Cross in Gold awarded on 25 November 1943

The pilots of JG 1 clearly had a field day, submitting claims for no fewer than 13 bombers shot down (with other successes being credited to IV./NJG 1 and the Flak arm). The Bf 109 pilots enjoyed the lion's share with eight, but among the five Fw 190 claimants was Hauptmann Günther Specht of 10. *Staffel*, who shot a B-17 – probably of the 91st BG – into the North Sea some 50 miles to the northwest of Borkum, the westernmost of the German Frisian Islands, shortly after midday.

This aircraft was Specht's seventh confirmed victory, with his first two having been claimed over the German Bight during the opening months of the war. Then an oberleutnant flying Bf 109Ds with I./ZG 26 'Horst Wessel', Specht had despatched two RAF Hampdens southeast of Heligoland on 29 September 1939. In a running fight with a formation of Wellingtons over the same area on 3 December 1939, Specht was himself shot down and badly injured, losing the sight of one eye. Despite this disability he had returned to operational flying, and would rise to become one of the Defence of the Reich's leading personalities.

The Wilhelmshaven raid of 26 February brought to a close the first month of the Defence of the Reich campaign. With the benefit of informed hindsight, the balance sheet appears to be firmly in favour of the Luftwaffe. In the three engagements fought the Eighth Air Force had lost 15 heavy bombers, while its main adversary, JG 1, had suffered seven pilots killed and one wounded. The Americans' belief in unescorted daylight precision bombing had not yet been entirely vindicated, but neither had it yet been dented. During this first month, however, the Eighth had merely pecked at the northernmost periphery of Hitler's Reich. The real test would come later in the year when the 'heavies' started to venture further inland.

Their failure to penetrate deeper into Germany had not been for want of trying. And on 4 March, at their third attempt to attack the Hamm marshalling yards, they finally succeeded – or at least partially so. The weather gods must have taken their eye off the ball, for one of the four B-17 groups managed to find its way across the Low Countries on instruments and emerge into clear air over the target area. The 91st BG was to pay dearly for its perseverance, losing four of the five bombers shot down that day.

The defenders had been reinforced on this occasion not only by elements of III./JG 1 hurriedly transferred down from southern Norway, but also by nearly two-dozen Fw 190s of JG 26 that had taken up temporary residence alongside II./JG 1 at Woensdrecht. It was JG 1 which was credited with all the successes, its pilots claiming no fewer than ten B-17s, including two *Herausschüsse* and one 'final destruction'.

These last two terms perhaps require brief explanation. Luftwaffe fighter pilots were awarded their medals and decorations on the basis of a 'points' system. Shooting down an enemy single-engined fighter, for example, had long earned the victor one point (and, incidentally, the Iron Cross, Second Class). The advent of the US heavy bombers in the late summer of 1942 meant that this system had to be revised and expanded. The destruction of a four-engined bomber was clearly a much more difficult task than that of despatching a fighter.

It was therefore decided that the shooting down of an American heavy bomber merited three points (and an automatic Iron Cross, First Class).

Two other levels of 'success' against these formidable new opponents were introduced at the same time. An *Herausschuss* – literally meaning a 'shooting-out' – was the act of damaging a bomber so badly that it was forced to leave the relative safety of its combat box and drop out of formation. Such a 'shooting-out' – a 'separation' might be a better description – gained the pilot responsible two points.

A 'final destruction', as the name implies, was the subsequent downing of a previous *Herausschuss*. Unless it had been fortunate enough to acquire a fighter escort along the way (a benefit unavailable to the Eighth's pioneering bomber groups during their early forays into German airspace), any such lone straggler, limping home severely damaged across enemy-occupied territory, was little more than a sitting duck. The Luftwaffe fighter pilot who chanced upon it and delivered the *coup de grace* was deemed to have earned himself just one point.

The attack on Hamm by the 91st BG on 4 March had been the Eighth Air Force's first appearance over Germany's industrial heartland of the Ruhr. The Americans would challenge the Reich's defences only twice more before the end of the month, and the targets on both occasions were U-boat yards on or near the North Sea coast. The raid on the Vulkan yards at Bremen-Vegesack on 18 March resulted in JG 1's claiming seven US bombers shot down, although, in fact, only two were lost. It is not clear which of the three claimants for a B-17 brought down the single Flying Fortress, but the sole B-24 that failed to return from Vegesack almost certainly fell victim to Leutnant Hans Pancritius of 8./JG 1. The Liberator was 'Pankraz' Pancritius' second heavy bomber victory, for he had been credited with a B-17 destroyed during the Hamm raid two weeks earlier. And on 22 March, when all six of the Eighth Air Force's groups targeted the KM U-boat yards at Wilhelmshaven, he added a third by sending a B-24 down into the North Sea off the Dutch coast.

No black-and-white photograph can properly convey the savage fury of a fighter assault on a formation of bombers. Here, this otherwise innocuous collection of dots *does* graphically illustrate an *Herausschuss*. With a fighter closing in for a second pass, an already-stricken Flying Fortress starts to go down trailing smoke. Some sources suggest that the bomber may be a 95th BG machine lost during one of the Eighth's many visits to Bremen

Although the Eighth lost only three bombers during the Wilhelmshaven mission of 22 March – not the six claimed by JG 1 – the defenders were still holding their own. The Luftwaffe High Command was fully aware, however, that it would not be long before additional heavy bomber groups would be sent to the UK to add their weight to the American daylight bombing campaign against the Reich. It was to counter this perceived threat that a new *Jagdgeschwader* was added to the aerial defences of the North Sea coastal belt.

Strictly speaking, it would be more accurate to say that those defences were increased from the four existing *Jagdgruppen* to six. Ever since the days of the original *Fliegergruppe* Döberitz – Charles Lindbergh's hosts of seven years before – it had been standard procedure for the Luftwaffe fighter arm to expand its numbers by creating new from old. A cadre would be hived off from a *Jagdgruppe* already in being to provide the nucleus for a new unit. And this is precisely what happened at the end of March 1943 when JG 1's four component *Gruppen* were split into two, and a third *Gruppe* was added to each pair to produce two *Jagdgeschwader* out of the one.

The two Fw 190 *Gruppen* of the original JG 1 that were taken over into the 'reconstituted' JG 1 as of 1 April 1943 were Major Fritz Losigkeit's IV./JG 1, which now became the new I./JG 1, and Major Herbert Kijewski's II./JG 1, which retained its existing designation. The third Fw 190 *Gruppe* of the old JG 1, Major Walter Spies' III./JG 1, was redesignated to become the first *Gruppe* of new *Jagdgeschwader* JG 11, while the Bf 109s of the hitherto I./JG 1 would now operate as II./JG 11.

The two additional *Gruppen* formed from scratch, III./JG 1 and III./JG 11, were both equipped with Bf 109s. The two new Defence of the Reich *Jagdgeschwader* thus comprised a mix of three Bf 109 *Gruppen* and three Fw 190 *Gruppen*, the latter being I. and II./JG 1, and I./JG 11.

The officer appointed to command the 'new' JG 1 was the highly successful Major Hans Philipp, previously the *Gruppenkommandeur* of I./JG 54 on the eastern front. Already wearing the Oak Leaves with Swords, 'Fips' Philipp had scored his 200th victory just two weeks earlier. He was only the second Luftwaffe fighter pilot to rack up a double century. Philipp's counterpart at the head of JG 11 was equally experienced. Dalmatian-born Major Anton Mader had entered the Luftwaffe at the time of the integration of the Austrian air arm in 1938. Latterly, he too had been serving as a *Gruppenkommandeur*, commanding II./JG 77 in North Africa, although his personal score stood at a more modest 65.

The Defence of the Reich campaign to date had been something of a private war between the six pioneering heavy bomber groups of the Eighth Air Force and the pilots of the original JG 1. Now with the two *Jagdgeschwader* deployed shoulder-to-shoulder along the North Sea coastal belt – JG 1 occupying bases in the Netherlands and JG 11 stationed in northwest Germany – the battle was about to enter a new phase.

The strengthening of the Luftwaffe's defences could not have occurred at a more opportune moment. The Eighth made just one incursion into Reich airspace in April, and it came up against the strongest fighter opposition so far encountered in the campaign, resulting in the day's losses being more than double those of any previous mission. It also gave

Shown here wearing the Oak Leaves with Swords, the 203-victory Major Hans Philipp was transferred back from Russia to take command of the 'new' JG 1 on 1 April 1943. He scored just three kills while at the head of the *Geschwader* – a Spitfire on 2 May, a P-47 on 16 May and a Flying Fortress on 8 October 1943

Philipp's counterpart at JG 11 was Major Anton Mader, seen (left) in conversation with Major Karl-Heinz Leesmann, first *Kommandeur* of the Bf 109-equipped III./JG 1 (who would be killed in action on 25 July 1943). Mader claimed three B-17s as *Geschwaderkommodore* of JG 11 before being appointed to the command of JG 54 on the eastern front in January 1944

rise to the first serious doubts as to the viability of unescorted daylight bomber operations.

The 17 April raid was a return visit to Bremen by the Eighth's four B-17 groups. This time, however, the objective was not the Vegesack submarine yards but – more symbolically perhaps – the city's Focke-Wulf aircraft factories, which were producing the very Fw 190 fighters that the Americans were facing in the air. And it was the Fw 190 *Gruppen* of JGs 1 and 11 that inflicted the most damage on the attackers.

For once the Luftwaffe pilots' claims very nearly tallied with their enemy's admitted losses. Sixteen Flying Fortresses failed to return – just one less than the 17 credited to the defending fighters. Ten of the B-17s fell to Fw 190s, with one of the claimants being Major Fritz Losigkeit. It was the *Gruppenkommandeur's* sixth victory of the war, and his first heavy bomber. Leutnant Pancritius, now of 2./JG 11, went one better by downing a brace of B-17s. This took his total of US bombers destroyed to five, which effectively made him the first *Viermot* (four-engined) ace of the Defence of the Reich campaign.

The only fatality suffered by the two *Geschwader* was 3./JG 1's Unteroffizier Hans Pelzer, whose Focke-Wulf was shot down south of Bremen. Another Fw 190 was damaged in an emergency landing, as were four Bf 109s, together with a fifth that crashed after being damaged in combat. Even so, this still fell far short of the 63 Luftwaffe fighters destroyed, plus 15 probables, that were claimed by the embattled Flying Fortress gunners!

Given the 15 percent losses sustained during the Bremen mission, it is perhaps not surprising that very nearly a month was to pass before the Eighth reappeared over the Reich. The target for the raid of 14 May was the submarine yards at Kiel. By this time three more B-17 groups had been added to the Eighth's order of battle, although only one of these participated in the mission to Kiel. Fw 190 pilots submitted claims for three B-17s destroyed, again at the cost of just one of their number, Feldwebel Karl Thon of 3./JG 11 going down into the Baltic north of the target area.

The following day saw a maximum effort involving all nine B-17 groups, five being despatched against Wilhelmshaven and four striking at Emden. The former encountered solid cloud and so bombed targets of opportunity in the German Bight region. Five Flying Fortresses failed to make it back across the North Sea, I./JG 11 claiming two of them, one of which provided 'Pankraz' Pancritius with his number six. The Emden force lost just one machine, although three of I./JG 11's pilots submitted claims. Exactly who sent the 351st BG Flying Fortress spiralling into the sea northwest of Borkum is open to question, but it seems unlikely to have been the Feldwebel who identified his victim as a Short Stirling!

Before the month was out the Eighth mounted two further missions against U-boat yards in northern Germany. On 19 May the Americans

Feldwebel – later Leutnant – Alwin Doppler of JG 11 would rise to become the second-highest scoring Fw 190 Defence of the Reich *Viermot-Töter* (four-engined bomber killer) with a final total of 25 US 'heavies' to his credit before being killed in Operation *Bodenplatte*, the Luftwaffe's last-ditch attack on Allied airfields in France and the Low Countries on New Year's Day 1945

struck at Kiel and Flensburg, and the casualties they suffered on this date were all inflicted by Bf 109s. Forty-eight hours later the same nine groups of B-17s targeted Wilhelmshaven and Emden once again, and this time the Fw 190 *Gruppen* were more successful, being credited with five of the 13 bombers downed.

Two of the B-17s were claimed by pilots of 2./JG 11. One of them was the third heavy bomber victory for future *Viermot* ace Feldwebel Alwin Doppler, who had scored a kill on each of the Eighth's last two visits to Wilhelmshaven (on 26 February and 22 March). The other took Leutnant Pancritius' tally to seven. I./JG 1 claimed three B-17s, but it cost the unit the *Kapitän* of 1. *Staffel*, Oberleutnant Hans Munz, who was downed off the Dutch coast. He was seen descending by parachute, and although an exact fix of the position had been taken, an exhaustive air-sea rescue search found only an empty dinghy. Munz's body was washed ashore on the island of Sylt six weeks later.

It was 11 June before the Eighth's B-17s next entered Reich airspace, and once again Wilhelmshaven was among the targets attacked. JGs 1 and 11 were credited with 14 of the 22 Flying Fortresses claimed shot down, of which just three went to Fw 190s. Two days later it was a different story, with the USAAF 'heavies' performing simultaneous raids on the U-boat yards at Bremen and Kiel. The larger Bremen force, comprising seven groups of B-17s, escaped relatively lightly. Retiring from the target area, they were intercepted off the coast by the Focke-Wulfs of I./JG 1. Four of the bombers went down, which matches exactly the four claims submitted by the Fw 190s. Two of the four B-17s were credited to veteran NCO pilot Oberfeldwebel Hans Laun.

The defending Luftwaffe fighters concentrated most of their attention on the three groups of Flying Fortresses heading for Kiel and gave them a savage mauling. The Americans admitted the loss of 22 bombers – nearly a third of the number despatched. JGs 1 and 11 claimed 14 of them, six of which fell victim to Fw 190s. The now Oberleutnant Pancritius accounted for a pair of B-17s, which took his growing four-engined tally to nine (although the second was subsequently disallowed). At day's end the Luftwaffe reported the destruction of 34 bombers.

The Eighth's actual losses were not far short of this figure and, when taken together with the 54 bombers that returned to base damaged, this constituted a significant setback to the Americans' daylight offensive. It was certainly serious enough to warrant a change of strategy. The USAAF decided that no further raids would be mounted over the German Bight area until the Eighth's P-47 escort fighters could be fitted with long-range fuel tanks. These would enable them to accompany the bombers beyond the Low Countries and across the border at least into the northwesternmost fringes of the Reich (roughly along an arc running from Emden through Dortmund and down to Koblenz).

Yet despite this stricture, the Americans risked another unescorted foray into Germany just over a week later. The target for the ten groups of B-17s on 22 June was the synthetic rubber plant at Hüls. It was the first time the Eighth had been back to the Ruhr since the 91st BG's solo effort against Hamm marshalling yards on 4 March. The Flying Fortresses did not escape lightly from this, their first major raid on the Ruhr industrial basin. They were intercepted east of Wesel, just beyond the Dutch border, by the Fw 190s of I./JG 1. In the space of some 35 minutes the Focke-Wulfs claimed 14 of the bombers destroyed without loss to themselves. Oberfeldwebel Laun accounted for three of them (two being *Herausschüsse*), which increased his heavy bomber total to seven.

The B-17s then came under renewed attack, this time from II./JG 1, as they retired out over the Low Countries. By now they had made rendezvous with the fighters waiting to escort them home, and only one further bomber went down. This was credited to Oberleutnant Harry Koch, the *Staffelkapitän* of 6./JG 1. Although the Eighth had suffered serious losses, it had inflicted major damage on the Hüls plant. It is estimated that this one raid alone cost the Germans ten percent of their total annual production of synthetic rubber.

Instead of returning to Hüls to finish the job, as the Germans feared they might, the Eighth's bombers next revisited their old stamping grounds in the north again. Bad weather and heavy cloud prevented the 13 groups of B-17s from reaching their assigned targets on this 25 June, however. The adverse conditions also forced their escorting fighters to

A B-17 of the 305th BG over Hüls on 22 June 1943. The serial number of the machine is indecipherable on the original print, but could this be the KY-M (aka *Mary T*) that was to be brought down near Aachen on 14 October 1943 – one of the 15 Flying Fortresses claimed by the Fw 190s of JG 1 in that area during 'Second Schweinfurt'?

Pictured in the cockpit of his
'White 20', Hauptmann Emil-Rudolf
Schnoor, the recently appointed
Gruppenkommandeur of I./JG 1,
claimed the third heavy bomber
of his career over Holland on
25 June 1943. The intertwined
'Double-M' beneath the windscreen
is his personal emblem – an oblique
reference to his home city of
Hamburg

turn back early – not that the P-47s could have accompanied their charges all the way to the original objectives. The day's maximum effort thus degenerated into a number of uncoordinated attacks on various targets of opportunity, including shipping convoys off the East Frisian Islands.

The thick clouds likewise hampered the Luftwaffe's defending fighters, but did not prevent their claiming over 30 heavy bombers – a good dozen more than the USAAF lost. The Fw 190s of I./JG 1 and I./JG 11 were together credited with a total of eight Flying Fortresses, one of them, sent down southeast of Groningen, in Holland, being the third heavy bomber victory for I./JG 1's *Gruppenkommandeur*, Hauptmann Emil-Rudolf Schnoor. Two others helped boost the totals of the two pilots currently heading the list of *Viermot* aces, with a tenth kill being credited to Oberleutnant Pancritius of 2./JG 11 and an eighth to 1./JG 1's Oberfeldwebel Laun.

The scattered attacks of 25 June brought to an end the first half of 1943. The opening rounds of the Defence of the Reich campaign had produced mixed results. After a tentative start by both sides, the burgeoning strength and confidence of the defending fighters had seen them take an ever-increasing toll of American bombers, from just three over Wilhelmshaven on 27 January to no fewer than 26 during the Bremen and Kiel missions of 13 June. For their part, the Americans had more than doubled their numbers, the six original bomb groups of January growing to 13 by mid-June. And at Hüls they had demonstrated just how much damage they were capable of inflicting. Although still very faint, the writing was undoubtedly already on the wall.

The one overriding factor of all these early missions was the lack of a fighter escort for the enemy bomber formations. The concept of unescorted daylight bombing was hanging in the balance. The Americans were making frantic efforts to rectify the situation, but it would take time – time that the Luftwaffe would utilise to the full. The final outcome of the Defence of the Reich campaign was still far from certain.

During the second half of 1943 the pilots of JGs 1 and 11 would continue to savage the bomber formations. The Eighth was to suffer catastrophic casualties on two days in particular during this period. Many more *Viermot* aces would emerge from the ranks of the Fw 190 *Gruppen*, but the defenders' own losses would also begin to escalate as the year ran its course.

Cause and effect – armourers prepare to load the contents of a fresh box of 2 cm (20 mm) cannon shells into the drum magazines (background) of a Focke-Wulf's wing guns . . .

. . . and an illustration of the damage these weapons could inflict on a heavy bomber. German officers inspect the shell-holed remains of the 384th BG's 'BK-F', which was one of the five B-17s this group lost during a mission over France on 26 June 1943. Some references suggest that the unnamed 42-30037, brought down between Dieppe and Le Tréport, was the 90th victory of the war (and the fifth heavy bomber) for Major Josef 'Pips' Priller, the *Geschwaderkommodore* of JG 26. In all, Priller would be credited with 11 four-engined bombers, only three of which were claimed during Defence of the Reich missions

SIGNAL VICTORIES AND GROWING LOSSES

During the latter half of 1943 the Eighth Air Force would fly nearly twice as many missions against the Reich, and in far greater numbers, than it had done during the first half of the year. July, however, began where June had left off, with the weather playing the dominant role in the proceedings. The assigned objectives for 17 July were Hamburg and Hannover, but both missions had to be recalled due to the adverse conditions. The B-17s resorted to attacking targets of opportunity, and although nine *Jagdgruppen* were sent up against them, the Luftwaffe's pilots had a hard time finding the widely scattered bomber formations. They later submitted claims for 14 bombers, although the Americans in fact lost only two.

There were just two Fw 190 claimants on this date – one a member of I./JG 26 and the other the recently appointed *Gruppenkommandeur* of I./JG 11, Hauptmann Erwin Clausen. The Oak Leaves-wearing Clausen had recently been serving as a *Staffelkapitän* in a fighter-training wing (JGr.Süd), prior to which he had spent almost his entire operational career with JG 77. The Flying Fortress he downed on 17 July – his first heavy bomber – was his 121st victory overall. I./JG 11 paid a heavy price for its single kill, as the *Gruppe* lost its most successful *Viermot* specialist, Oberleutnant Hans Pancritius. His 'Yellow 12' was shot down while attacking a formation of B-17s north of the island of Borkum.

The Eighth's next incursion into North German airspace on 25 July also encountered heavy cloud, which again forced the bombers to dissipate their efforts against targets of opportunity. The Fw 190s of II./JG 1 and I./JG 11 claimed six Flying Fortresses downed, with Oberleutnant Harry Koch, the *Staffelkapitän* of 6./JG 1, and Hauptmann Erwin Clausen of I./JG 11 each adding a second heavy bomber to their total scores.

The same two pilots were among the successful claimants the following day when conditions finally allowed the Eighth to strike at its primary targets – the U-boat

The Oak Leaves-wearing Oberleutnant Erwin Clausen (centre) enjoys a spot of home leave. He assumed command of I./JG 11 on 20 June 1943, downing his first heavy bomber less than a month later. He was to add 11 more before being reported missing in action on 4 October 1943

yards in Hamburg and two synthetic rubber plants in Hannover. The great port city of Hamburg was still reeling from the first of the series of RAF Bomber Command night raids, which were to culminate in the horrific firestorm of 27/28 July. It was the Hannover formation that bore the brunt of the Luftwaffe's day fighter attacks, losing 16 Flying Fortresses to the Hamburg force's two. Luftwaffe claims for the day totalled 33, with the three Focke-Wulf *Gruppen* of JGs 1 and 11 accounting for 16 of them. In addition to Erwin Clausen (who was credited with a pair of bombers) and Harry Koch, two other future four-engined *Experten* – 1./JG 1's Leutnant Rudolf Engleder and 2./JG 11's Feldwebel Alwin Doppler – downed a B-17 apiece on this date.

Hauptmann Clausen repeated his performance by adding another brace of Flying Fortresses to his score on 28 July – the day that the Eighth targeted the Fieseler and AGO aircraft works at Kassel and Oschersleben, respectively. This took the *Kommandeur's* tally of heavy bombers to six. Fifteen other Fw 190 pilots (including two from I./JG 26) claimed a bomber each. Alwin Doppler also achieved ace status by downing his fifth, while Oberfeldwebel Hans Laun of 3./JG 1, who had inherited the late 'Pankraz' Pancritius' mantle as the most successful *Viermot*-killer of the campaign to date, raised his total to nine.

In addition to these personal milestones, the raids of 28 July were noteworthy for two other factors. It was reportedly the first occasion that the Luftwaffe's single-engined fighters had successfully employed underwing rockets against the American bomber formations. And it was the first time that USAAF fighters had entered German airspace. Admittedly, the latter could not yet penetrate far beyond the border, as the P-47s' new jettisonable fuel tanks afforded them only an additional 30 miles' radius of action, but it did mean that the Eighth's fighters would henceforth be able to rendezvous with the returning bombers well in time to escort them back through the hostile skies of Holland.

The following day, however, it was once again the weather that was to prove the bombers' best protection when, on 29 July, 15 groups of B-17s attacked two targets on the Baltic coast – the U-boat yards at Kiel and the Arado aircraft works at Warnemünde. The Luftwaffe's response was relatively low-key, with only four *Jagdgruppen*, including the Husum-based Fw 190s of I./JG 11, being scrambled to oppose them. The Focke-Wulf *Gruppe* was credited with four of the 12 bombers claimed shot down (which matched exactly the Americans' admitted combat losses). The *Kommandeur*, Hauptmann Clausen, got his now seemingly obligatory pair, while Leutnant Heinrich Rudolph also achieved a double. The four bombers, probably of the 306th BG, all went down within the space of 15 minutes shortly after leaving the target area at Kiel.

Twenty-four hours later the B-17s were back over the Reich, heading inland for a second strike against Fieseler's aircraft factories in Kassel. This time the Luftwaffe's fighters reacted with more vigour. Among the 11 *Jagdgruppen* sent up in opposition were at least five Fw 190 units, namely I. and II./JG 1, III./JG 2 and I. and II./JG 26, the latter pair having recently transferred up to Holland from their more traditional hunting grounds over northeast France.

JG 26, like JG 2, was subordinated to *Luftflotte* 3 – the air fleet deployed primarily across occupied northwest Europe – and, as such, was not

strictly speaking an integral part of the Defence of the Reich organisation proper. Nevertheless, both these western-based *Jagdgeschwader* would find themselves increasingly involved in homeland defence operations as the American daylight bombing offensive came to dominate the air war in Europe.

The Focke-Wulfs of JG 1 did not engage the bombers until they had long departed the target area and were about to re-cross the Dutch border and meet up with the Allied fighters tasked with escorting them back to the UK. The appearance on the scene of enemy fighters added a whole new dimension to the Defence of the Reich campaign. It meant that the Luftwaffe's pilots could no longer concentrate their entire attention upon the bomber formations in front of them, lining them up in their sights and launching their assaults without having to give heed to their backs. No longer could they be guaranteed the luxury of choosing when and where attack the bombers, secure in the knowledge that they were safe until they came within range of their targets' own gunners.

For the moment the very real threat posed by Allied fighters only existed close to Germany's western borders, but it was a threat that would grow over the months ahead until, ultimately, no corner of the Reich would be immune from their presence.

Despite this unwelcome development, I./JG 1 was able to claim six Flying Fortresses and two enemy fighters destroyed. These successes came at a very high price, however, for the *Gruppe* lost seven aircraft. Among the pilots killed were two *Staffelkapitäne* and the campaign's then leading Fw 190 *Viermot* ace, Oberfeldwebel Hans Laun of 1./JG 1, who was shot down near Arnhem.

At Rheine II./JG 1 had managed to get only six machines into the air. The unit had suffered a single casualty and its sole success was a Flying

An unidentified II. *Gruppe* pilot describes how it is done for the benefit of the propaganda company news cameraman kneeling left (and to the obvious amusement of his mechanic in the centre). Are those eloquent hand movements describing a dogfight or the curving in to make a classic 'twelve-o'clock high' attack on an enemy bomber?

Fortress straggler caught and despatched by the *Kapitän* of 6. *Staffel*, Oberleutnant Harry Koch.

The two Dutch-based *Gruppen* of JG 26 submitted claims for seven Flying Fortresses and four fighters. *Gruppenkommandeur* of II./JG 26, Major Wilhelm-Ferdinand Galland – a younger brother of *General der Flieger* Adolf Galland – sent one B-17 down east of Apeldoorn. It was 'Wutz' Galland's 53rd victory overall, and although he had already been credited with six other heavy bombers during earlier encounters over France and the Low Countries, this was the first of his victims to have been engaged in an attack on the Reich.

The day also provided the first Defence of the Reich bomber victory for the man who developed and introduced the frontal attack method of combating the American four-engined bomber formations, Major Egon Mayer, *Geschwaderkommodore* of JG 2. The Flying Fortress credited to Mayer on this date made him a heavy bomber ace three times over, but all 14 of his previous such victories had been achieved during Eighth Air Force attacks on targets in France.

The 30 July mission against Kassel was the final operation of the USAAF's so-called 'Blitz Week', whose aim it had been to test the Luftwaffe's fighter defences to the limit by mounting seven maximum-effort bombing raids over seven consecutive days. It may well have succeeded in this aim (as witness II./JG 1 being able to scramble just six of its Focke-Wulfs) but, given the fledgling nature of the Eighth's available escort fighter force, the experiment was considered by some to have been a trifle premature.

It had certainly been expensive, for 87 bombers had been lost and well over 500 damaged – the vast majority as a result of attack by Luftwaffe fighters. Perhaps the most telling verdict on 'Blitz Week' was the fact that the Eighth's heavy bomber groups stood down for the next 12 days. It did them little good, for although only two raids were to be mounted against the Reich during August, they alone would cost the Americans

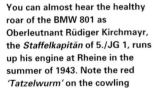

You can almost hear the healthy roar of the BMW 801 as Oberleutnant Rüdiger Kirchmayr, the *Staffelkapitän* of 5./JG 1, runs up his engine at Rheine in the summer of 1943. Note the red *'Tatzelwurm'* on the cowling

a further 85 bombers – just two short of the total lost throughout the whole of 'Blitz Week'.

The twin strikes of 12 August, aimed at targets in the Ruhr and Rhine regions, again faced bad weather, with almost unbroken cloud covering western Germany's border provinces. This did not prevent 11 *Jagdgruppen* (including four Fw 190 units) from scrambling to engage the enemy, however. The Focke-Wulfs of JGs 1 and 26 claimed a total of 24 Flying Fortresses, shared equally between the two *Geschwader*. Coincidentally, each *Geschwader* also lost a single pilot killed in action against the bombers' escorting P-47s, which were equipped for the first time with new, pressurised belly tanks.

Among JG 1's claimants were Hauptmann Emil-Rudolf Schnoor, the *Kommandeur* of I. *Gruppe*, and Oberleutnant Harry Koch, the *Kapitän* of 6. *Staffel*, both of whom racked up their fifth Flying Fortress kills on this date. Another B-17 provided the first *Viermot* victory for Hauptmann Walter Hoeckner, who had recently been appointed *Gruppenkommandeur* of II./JG 1. He already had 56 enemy aircraft under his belt, all but four of them Russian.

Among the ranks of JG 26, Major Wilhelm-Ferdinand Galland, the *Kommandeur* of II. *Gruppe*, downed his fourth (and last) four-engined bomber in Defence of the Reich, while one of his most successful NCO pilots, the 37-victory Oberfeldwebel Adolf 'Addi' Glunz of 4. *Staffel*, opened his Reich's Defence scoreboard with a brace of B-17s. Another future ace to claim his first Defence of the Reich bomber on this date was 3./JG 26's Feldwebel Erich Scheyda. In total, Luftwaffe pilots claimed 37 enemy aircraft destroyed. Although the Eighth's actual losses were 'only' 25, this still represented the second highest casualty rate of the campaign to date (surpassed only by the 26 bombers lost on the Bremen-Kiel missions of 13 June). This tally paled into insignificance when compared with what came next, for five days later the Flying Fortresses were sent to Schweinfurt and Regensburg.

Major Egon Mayer, the *Geschwaderkommodore* of JG 2, is seen here (in shorts) standing on top of one of his victims. Like 'Pips' Priller of JG 26, most of Mayer's heavy bomber successes were claimed during Eighth Air Force missions against targets in occupied northwest Europe rather than within the Reich itself. This is one such, the 94th BG's *'Nip n' Tuck'* (QE-W/42-3190), which bellied in on a French farmer's cornfield near Evreux on 14 July 1943

Mission No 84 of 17 August 1943 would be the Eighth Air Force's most daring and ambitious operation of the campaign to date. Its objectives – the ball bearing manufacturing plants at Schweinfurt and the Messerschmitt aircraft factory at Regensburg – lay deep inside Germany. The two target areas were just over 100 miles apart and the twin attacks would be coordinated in an effort to split the Luftwaffe's defending fighter forces. As had so often been the case in the past, the weather took a hand. Conditions were perfect all across northwest Europe, except over the Americans' heavy bomber bases in the UK, which were blanketed in low mist and cloud.

The seven B-17 groups of the Regensburg force could not afford to delay for long, however, for after bombing the Messerschmitt works they were not heading back to their bases in England but would instead continue south over the Alps and across the Mediterranean to land in North Africa. And for this they needed daylight. After waiting an hour they had to take off, despite the appalling conditions, or risk jeopardising the entire operation. But then the Schweinfurt force, nine groups in all, had to be held on the ground for a further three-and-a-half hours, waiting not only for the weather to improve, but also for the fighters that were escorting the Regensburg formation across Belgium to return to their UK bases to refuel and rearm.

The elaborate plan had fallen to pieces. In place of the coordinated strike, the mission now consisted of two completely separate bomber formations, one trailing the other along almost the same route into Germany – and with a dangerous time lapse between the two. It was a situation the Luftwaffe's experienced fighter controllers could not fail to seize upon. The *Jagdgruppen* would be able to engage the first force and then land, refuel and rearm, ready to intercept the bombers on their return flight – and then repeat the entire process against the second force.

The Regensburg formations' course across northern Belgium was to take them perilously close to Woensdrecht airfield in neighbouring Holland, which then housed the Fw 190s of II./JG 1 and I./JG 26. The latter *Gruppe* was the first to be scrambled in what proved to be a precautionary measure before the B-17s had even reached the mainland coast. It was I./JG 26's *Kommandeur*, Hauptmann Karl Borris, who was to claim the first of the 60 Flying Fortresses lost by the Eighth on this disastrous day, his victim going down 20 miles to the east of Louvain. Three of Borris' pilots also submitted claims for a B-17 apiece.

After leaving Belgium (and their P-47 escort) behind, the bombers enjoyed a relatively clear run until reaching the Rhine south of Darmstadt. Here, they were confronted by a fresh wave of Luftwaffe interceptors, including a formation of Fw 190s from Hauptmann Schnoor's Deelen-based I./JG 1. Among the five B-17s claimed by the *Gruppe* during the

Appointed *Gruppenkommandeur* of II./JG 1 on 26 June 1943, Hauptmann Walter Hoeckner got the first of his six Defence of the Reich heavy bombers – probably a machine of the 92nd BG – northwest of Apeldoorn, in Holland, on 12 August 1943

No doubt about the identity of the first Defence of the Reich heavy bomber credited to Hauptmann Karl Borris, the *Gruppenkommandeur* of I./JG 26. The B-17 he sent down east-northeast of Louvain, Belgium, on 17 August 1943 – *'Dear Mom'* of the 94th BG (QE-Z/42-30389) – was also the first of the 60 Flying Fortresses lost on that day's disastrous Schweinfurt/Regensburg mission. Borris just missed out on becoming a Reich anti-bomber ace as one of the five B-17s included in his final score had been targeting the French Renault works outside Paris

30-minute fight that ensued were two (one of them an *Herausschuss*) for future *Viermot* ace Leutnant Hans Ehlers of 2. *Staffel*.

The Focke-Wulfs had thus been credited with nine of the 14 Flying Fortresses downed en route to Regensburg. Now it was time for the German fighters to land and take on fresh fuel and ammunition ready to meet the bombers on their return flight. The Regensburg formation did not return, however – at least not on this date. The bombers continued on to North Africa, losing ten more of their number along the way. Yet the day's action was far from over for the Luftwaffe fighter pilots, as the Schweinfurt force had yet to put in an appearance. And when it did, it would run into an even greater concentration of fighters and suffer even heavier casualties than had been inflicted on the Regensburg groups.

Oberfeldwebel Hans Ehlers (left) had already been credited with a B-17 over France while a member of 6./JG 1 – note the yellow *'Tatzelwurm'* – before being promoted to leutnant, transferred to 2./JG 1 and claiming his first two Defence of the Reich Fortresses (one of them an *Herausschuss*) during 'First Schweinfurt'

This shot of the hectic activity surrounding a *Geschwader*-Adjutant's machine – possibly Rolf Hermichen's – as it is re-armed and refuelled for a second mission gives a vivid impression of the race against time to get the aircraft back into the air

In fact, the 14 *Jagdgruppen* – plus elements of other nightfighter, flying school and factory defence units – that awaited the arrival of the Schweinfurt bombers constituted the largest fighter defence force yet assembled in the Defence of the Reich campaign.

Woensdrecht's Focke-Wulfs were again in the forefront of the action, with I./JG 26 being credited with four more B-17s destroyed. Two of the unit's pilots, Oberleutnant Artur Beese, the *Staffelkapitän* of 1./JG 26, and Feldwebel Peter Ahrens of 3. *Staffel*, each added a second Flying Fortress to the ones that they had shot out of the Regensburg force just over three hours earlier. This time II./JG 1, which had been kept on the ground when the Regensburg bombers flew overhead during the morning, also entered the fray. Its pilots claimed four B-17s – one of them providing 5. *Staffel's* Oberfeldwebel Otto Bach with his fifth – plus two *Herausschüsse*.

It was the next stage, from the Belgian border to the Rhine, which was to witness the day's fiercest action. Unlike the Regensburg B-17s, which had traversed this leg almost without hindrance, the Schweinfurt-bound bombers found themselves under attack from as many as nine *Jagdgruppen* at a time. Among them were two Fw 190 units scrambled from Arnhem-Deelen, namely the refuelled and rearmed I./JG 1, and Hauptmann Erwin Clausen's I./JG 11, which had flown in from Husum up on Germany's North Sea coast. The Fw 190 pilots claimed 14 bombers, divided equally between the two *Gruppen*. I./JG 1's seven confirmed kills raised its tally for the day to 12, while true to recent form, Kommandeur Erwin Clausen contributed a brace of B-17s to I./JG 11's seven victories, which also included a first for future *Viermot* ace Feldwebel Heinz Stöwer of 3. *Staffel*.

Still the aerial battle raged. The Americans had lost 24 bombers in total *before* reaching Schweinfurt. And now – unlike the Regensburg force, which had taken the Germans by surprise by disappearing southwards – they had to make the return flight back across Germany and Belgium in the face of defences that were thoroughly roused. This time, however, the Luftwaffe's fighter pilots were almost as exhausted by the protracted engagements as the enemy's bomber crews. The *Jagdgruppen* were no longer operating as cohesive units, with individual pilots putting down at the first airfield they could find as their red fuel warning lights began to glow. Despite this, another 12 Flying Fortresses would be lost before Mission No 84 was finally over.

In their third and final action of the day, pilots of I./JG 1 claimed three more B-17s. One of these, an *Herausschuss* north of Antwerp, was the fifth heavy bomber victory for 1. *Staffel's* Leutnant Rudolf Engleder. The badly mauled Schweinfurt force still had one last obstacle to face in the form of a fresh *Jagdgruppe* that had yet to play a part in the battle. Taking off from Lille-Nord in northeast France, Major Wilhelm-Ferdinand Galland's II./JG 26 joined up with the *Stabsschwarm* of JG 26 – led by

Another established *Experte* who opened his Defence of the Reich bomber score sheet on the day of 'First Schweinfurt' was the already-mentioned Oberstleutnant Josef Priller, *Geschwaderkommodore* of JG 26, who was responsible for one of the two Flying Fortresses shot down northwest of Liège during the bombers' return flight

the redoubtable Oberstleutnant Josef 'Pips' Priller – before heading east to attack the returning bomber stream head-on close to the German border near Liège.

The highly experienced Priller quickly sent a B-17 down in flames to crash at Tongeren, northwest of Liège. Although this was the *Geschwaderkommodore's* 92nd victory of the war, and his seventh heavy bomber kill, it was his first Defence of the Reich bomber success. Meanwhile, the pilots of II./JG 26 were so intent on reforming for a second pass at the Flying Fortresses that they failed entirely to notice that rendezvous had been made with the Americans' fighter escort. In fact, one P-47 group – the 56th FG, Col 'Hub' Zemke's famous 'Wolfpack' – had deliberately flown *past* the bombers in order to bounce the Focke-Wulfs from behind.

The ruse worked. Taken by surprise, the Fw 190s scattered in all directions. 'Wutz' Galland disappeared, the pilot who had been flying on his wing was wounded and a third member of the *Stabsschwarm*, Oberleutnant *Baron* Konrad von Donner, was forced to land his damaged machine at Brussels-Evère. The baron immediately commandeered a Bf 108 light aircraft and set off on an aerial search for his missing *Gruppenkommandeur*, but it was to no avail. Two months were to pass before the body of Major Wilhelm-Ferdinand Galland was found, still in the cockpit of his fighter, 14 miles to the north of Liège.

The sudden appearance of the P-47s had robbed II./JG 26 of any chance of carrying out another coordinated attack on the retiring bombers. Nevertheless, several of the *Gruppe's* pilots continued to stalk the B-17s, 4. *Staffel's* Oberfeldwebel Adolf Glunz claiming the last of the Schweinfurt force to be brought down on Belgian soil. His victim crashed at Averbode, 20 miles northeast of Brussels. And a 6. *Staffel* pilot was subsequently credited with one of the two Flying Fortresses that ditched in the North Sea.

Early P-47D Thunderbolts of the famous 56th FG . . .

... which bounced the Fw 190s of II./JG 26 near Liège, shooting down *Gruppenkommandeur* Major Wilhelm-Ferdinand Galland. Like fellow-*Kommandeur* Karl Borris of I./JG 26, 'Wutz' Galland's final tally of Defence of the Reich heavy bombers was four (out of a total of eight)

With Karl Borris having been credited with the first B-17 downed on 17 August 1943, it would fall to an NCO pilot of his 4. *Staffel*, Oberfeldwebel Adolf Glunz, to claim the last to come down on European soil on that fateful day (two would subsequently ditch in the Channel). 'Addi' Glunz's victim, the 305th BG's *'Patches'* (XK-W/41-24564), crashed some 20 miles outside Brussels. It was the third of the future ace's ten Defence of the Reich heavy bomber victories. This photograph does not show him returning from the mission, however, for he is clearly wearing the Knight's Cross awarded 12 days *after* 'First Schweinfurt'

So ended 'First Schweinfurt' (although, incredibly, the Eighth was to attack the same target again less than two months later and suffer equally grievous losses). The initial claims submitted by the German defences for enemy aircraft destroyed totalled 106, but after evaluation this figure was reduced, first to 71 and then to 61. This latter was remarkably accurate – the USAAF lost 60 bombers and three fighters in all – given that the Luftwaffe had little knowledge of the casualties suffered by the Regensburg force on its flight south after leaving the target area.

The Fw 190 *Gruppen* had escaped very lightly with just three fatalities (all from JG 26), although two of the nine pilots injured subsequently died of their wounds. The number of German fighters lost in action, or written off as a result of same, was 40 (including no less than 13 Bf 110s). Surviving USAAF aircrew claimed more than ten times that figure: 307 destroyed, 30 probables and 103 damaged – proof, if proof were needed, of the chaos and confusion surrounding the savage air battle that was 'First Schweinfurt'.

After the treatment meted out to the Americans on 17 August, it is perhaps not surprising that they did not venture back into Reich airspace for the best part of three weeks. In the interim they reorganised their bomber groups into three divisions – the 1st and 3rd flying B-17s, and the 2nd composed of the B-24s now returned from their two-month deployment to the Mediterranean theatre.

The Eighth's next foray into Germany was the 6 September mission to Stuttgart, which has since been described as 'one of the most costly fiascos in the Command's history'. On this occasion, however, their main opponent was not the Luftwaffe, but that old foe, the weather. Thick cloud fragmented the bombers' efforts and 45 B-17s failed to return, nearly half of them being forced to ditch or crash-land after running out of fuel. Few are recorded as having fallen to Fw 190s, although three were claimed by JG 2's Oberstleutnant Egon Mayer in the space of less than 20 minutes and a pair were credited to 3./JG 26's Feldwebel Erich Scheyda.

Another three weeks were to pass before the Flying Fortresses returned to Germany's skies. The mission of 27 September took them back to familiar territory – Emden on the North Sea coast – to face familiar adversaries: the fighters of JGs 1 and 11. However,

on this occasion the Luftwaffe pilots were in for a nasty surprise. For the first time, new 108 US gallon paper drop-tanks enabled USAAF fighters to escort the Eighth's bombers all the way to a target within the Reich.

All six *Gruppen* of the two *Jagdgeschwader* were scrambled, with I. and II./JG 11 being the first to sight and engage the enemy. With little experience of fighter-versus-fighter combat, the anti-bomber Bf 109s of II./JG 11 suffered badly – nine pilots were killed or posted missing and two wounded. I./JG 11 escaped much more lightly, with just one of its number missing. In compensation, the *Gruppe* downed a P-47 and a Flying Fortress. The latter fell to the *Kommandeur*, Hauptmann Erwin Clausen, who was also instrumental in (albeit not credited with) the demise of a second Thunderbolt. He chased the American fighter all the way down to sea level, only for it to hit the water and disappear beneath the surface before he could fire a single shot!

JG 1's part in the battle resulted in a single bomber *Herausschuss* for the loss of one pilot killed and one wounded. Altogether, the Luftwaffe claimed 15 bombers and three fighters. The Americans' true losses were seven and one respectively. This first fighter-versus-fighter confrontation over German territory during the Defence of the Reich campaign was thus anything but a resounding success for the defenders – the writing on that wall was becoming ever clearer.

In contrast to September's two incursions by the Eighth Air Force, the first half of October alone was to witness six raids on targets within Germany's borders, culminating in a second costly mission against Schweinfurt. Before that took place, however, the North Sea *Jagdgeschwader* suffered two grievous losses of their own.

Nearly 350 Flying Fortresses struck Emden again on 2 October. Just two bombers were lost, while their escorting fighters took a further heavy toll of JG 11's Messerschmitts. One of the B-17s was credited to future

Pilots of II./JG 26 take their ease during a lull between sorties. As the war progressed scenes of relative tranquility such as this would become increasingly rare

Fw 190 *Viermot* ace Leutnant Erich Hondt, the recently appointed *Staffelkapitän* of 2./JG 11. This was, in fact, Hondt's fifth heavy bomber victory, but the first four had all been claimed while flying Bf 109s.

Two days later, on 4 October, the B-17s' primary target was Frankfurt-am-Main. As a diversionary measure, a small force of B-24s was also sent out across the North Sea to 'trail their coats' off the Frisian Islands. The German Bight *Jagdgruppen* rose to the challenge, with the Focke-Wulfs of I./JG 11 claiming five of the Liberators – among them, one each for *Gruppenkommandeur* Hauptmann Erwin Clausen and the *Kapitän* of his 1. *Staffel*, Oberleutnant Heinz Sahnwaldt. They represented the two pilots' twelfth and first heavy bomber victories respectively, but they were also destined to be their last.

Hauptmann Clausen was in radio contact after the engagement, and although he reported that he was returning to base, neither he nor Heinz Sahnwaldt made it back to Husum. The reason for their disappearance remains unknown to this day. Although the vast bulk of Erwin Clausen's overall total of 132 victories had been scored on the eastern front, he could perhaps be regarded as the first 'major' Fw 190 pilot of the Defence of the Reich campaign to be lost.

Meanwhile, the B-17s heading for Frankfurt had been intercepted over the Rhine south of Koblenz by I. and II./JG 1. The Focke-Wulfs were credited with five bombers downed and two *Herausschüsse*. Due to a combination of circumstances, this was the last opposition the Flying Fortresses faced before reaching the target area, which they bombed virtually unimpeded. The good citizens of Frankfurt were incensed at the enemy's bombers being able to 'parade in formation across the sky as if taking part in a pre-war air pageant with not a single Luftwaffe fighter to be seen far or wide'. The district party leader, or Gauleiter, complained personally to Hitler, who berated Göring for the Luftwaffe's abysmal performance.

The Reichsmarschall in turn vented *his* displeasure on those *Jagdgruppen* engaged in Defence of the Reich operations and laid down a strict set of rules of engagement, which he insisted were to be followed in future (for more details see *Osprey Aircraft of the Aces 9 - Fw 190 Aces of the Western Front*, pp.9-10). This was one of the first signs of the growing rift that would open up between Göring and his senior fighter commanders during the final 18 months of the campaign.

And that campaign was clearly beginning to intensify. Starting on 8 October, the Americans launched three consecutive days of maximum-effort missions against targets within the Reich. The first of these was aimed at Bremen and neighbouring Vegesack, although intermittent cloud caused several formations to seek alternative targets of opportunity. The raids provoked a strong response from the Luftwaffe. Among the 11 *Gruppen* sent up against the bombers were the Focke-Wulfs of JGs 1 and 11. Under the temporary leadership of Oberleutnant Erich Hondt, I./JG 11 was again the first to engage. The encounter off the Dutch coast proved expensive, for although the *Gruppe* was able to claim three B-17s, two Fw 190 pilots were killed and Erich Hondt himself was seriously wounded.

I. and II./JG 1 fared far better when they intercepted the bombers closer to the target areas. They were subsequently credited with 20 Flying Fortresses destroyed, no fewer than eight of which were *Herausschüsse* (two of them taking the *Viermot* score of 1./JG 1's Unteroffizier Rudolf

2./JG 1's Feldwebel Anton-Rudolf Piffer got his fifth heavy bomber on 8 October 1943 when he downed a B-17 to the southwest of Bremen. He would go on to add 21 more to emerge as the most successful Fw 190 Defence of the Reich anti-bomber ace of all before being killed in a dogfight with P-51s over Normandy on 17 June 1944

The Eighth Air Force's mission to Bremen on 8 October may have brought heavy bomber acedom for 'Toni' Piffer, but it also resulted in the death of JG 1's *Geschwaderkommodore*, Oberstleutnant Hans Philipp. Seen here (right) earlier in his career wearing the three wings and bar of a hauptmann while welcoming a visiting Egon Mayer, Philipp was shot down in action against B-17s northwest of Rheine shortly after claiming his only heavy bomber

Hübl to five). Another B-17 provided the fifth heavy bomber for 2. *Staffel's* Oberfeldwebel Anton-Rudolf Piffer. It had cost them two pilots killed and three injured. Among the latter was Leutnant Hans Ehlers, who had been appointed *Kapitän* of 2. *Staffel* just one week earlier. He was forced to bail out of his 'Black 5' after ramming a Flying Fortress close to the Dutch border. This was the future ace's fourth heavy bomber of the Defence of the Reich campaign, his opening pair having been claimed during 'First Schweinfurt'.

There was one other fatality on 8 October – Oberstleutnant Hans Philipp, the *Geschwaderkommodore* of JG 1. 'Fips' Philipp had previously served as the *Kommandeur* of I./JG 54 on the eastern front. He had returned from Russia – wearing the Oak Leaves with Swords, and with a score of 203 victories – to assume command of the reconstituted JG 1 on 1 April 1943. Despite being a proven, natural and exemplary leader, it seems that Hans Philipp was never quite able to come to terms with homeland defence operations. The Flying Fortress that he claimed before being shot down himself just short of the Dutch border (according to one source by P-47s) was the only heavy bomber among his final total of 206 victories.

8 October had cost the Americans 30 bombers. The following day's strikes on Baltic coastal targets in eastern Germany and Poland saw them lose another 28. It was their longest mission of the campaign to date, which meant that it had to be flown without fighter escort. The Eighth's planners were relying on the element of surprise, plus a presumed paucity of defences that far to the east, to keep their losses within acceptable limits. In the event, the bombers came up against no fewer than nine *Jagdgruppen*, plus elements from five other twin-engined *Zerstörer* and nightfighter *Geschwader*.

The three Focke-Wulf *Gruppen* of JGs 1 and 11 engaged the bombers as they crossed the Schleswig-Holstein peninsula on both their outward and return flights, claiming a dozen B-17s downed and one *Herausschuss* for three pilots of their own (all from I./JG 11) killed or missing. The pair of Flying Fortresses credited to Hauptmann Schnoor, the *Kommandeur* of I./JG 1, took his score of heavy bombers to seven.

On 10 October the Eighth returned to western Germany with their first raid on Münster. The bombers were promised fighter cover all the way, but as so often in the past, the weather intervened, with fog keeping one of the planned relays of P-47 groups pinned to the ground at its UK base. The Luftwaffe fighter controllers, who were monitoring the incoming enemy formations and were already on top of the situation, swiftly took advantage of the gap in the Americans' fighter defences. A total of 11 *Jagdgruppen*, plus elements of at least six other single or twin-engined fighter units, had been brought to readiness. What followed has since been described as 'one of the most brutal and destructive air battles ever fought'. At its height '30 bombers and 26 Luftwaffe fighters' are said to have gone down in the space of less than 25 minutes.

Once again the Fw 190 *Gruppen* were at the forefront of the action, with I./JG 1 teaming up with I. and II./JG 26 to form a *Gefechtsverband*, or massed 'battle formation' – an early example of a practice that was to become increasingly common as the campaign progressed. The Focke-Wulfs launched their assault on the B-17s over the Dutch-German

Bombs burst in the wake of the 94th BG's *'Virgin's Delight'* during the strike against Marienburg on 9 October. This Fortress – more formally GL-V/42-3352 – would be shot into the North Sea by Luftwaffe fighters during a later raid on Bremen on 29 November 1943

border when the Americans were just minutes away from their target. In a succession of head-on attacks they wrought havoc among the leading bomb wing, which suffered 25 of the 30 bombers lost that day. One Flying Fortress group, the 'Bloody Hundredth' as it soon became known, was almost totally wiped out, losing all but one of its 13 B-17s.

Between them, the three Fw 190 *Gruppen* claimed a total of 13 bombers. The five credited to I./JG 1 included an *Herausschuss* for Oberleutnant Engleder, his tenth Defence of the Reich heavy bomber. These successes came at a cost of three pilots killed, however. JG 26's nine successes were achieved without loss. Among them was the first Flying Fortress to be added to the 54 previous victories of Major Johannes Seifert, the Knight's Cross-wearing *Gruppenkommandeur* of II./JG 26, and a fourth for 5. *Staffel's* Oberfeldwebel Adolf 'Addi' Glunz.

II./JG 1 engaged the bombers over the city of Münster itself. Led by Hauptmann Harry Koch, the *Staffelkapitän* of 6./JG 1, the *Gruppe* made its first pass at the B-17s just as they were releasing their bombs. Three Flying Fortresses went down immediately and a fourth dropped out of formation. One of the former was credited to the *Gruppenkommandeur*, Hauptmann Walter Hoeckner. However, the still relatively inexperienced Hoeckner, most of whose 59 previous kills had been scored in Russia, was hit by return fire and he was forced to bail out.

Subsequent attacks netted II./JG 1 five more bombers, the last providing the second *Herausschuss* of the day for Harry Koch. Altogether, the defenders submitted claims for 50 enemy aircraft destroyed, plus a further 22 probables. The Eighth's actual losses were 30 B-17s and a single P-47 fighter.

There appears to be a last-minute technical problem with the *Gruppenkommandeur's* machine (some sources suggest one flown by JG 2's Egon Mayer) as the wingman's aircraft prepares to taxi away from dispersal

Despite the savaging meted out to its crews over the past three days – 88 bombers missing and many more damaged or written off – the Eighth Air Force's planners were fully resolved to mount a fourth maximum effort on 11 October: a return visit to Schweinfurt, no less! Fortunately, perhaps, their intentions were thwarted by the weather. But they were nothing if not determined, and 72 hours later announced that conditions were at last right for a second raid on Schweinfurt. In this they were sadly mistaken. The poor weather was to play a significant part in the mission of 14 October, but it would be the Luftwaffe's fighters – in the largest numbers yet encountered – that hammered the final nails into the coffin of the unescorted daylight-bombing offensive.

Sixteen groups of B-17s, some 300 bombers in all (plus two-dozen Liberators carrying out another ineffectual diversionary foray across the North Sea), were despatched to bomb Schweinfurt. They would be faced by a staggering 20 *Jagdgruppen*, backed up by units from three *Zerstörer*, six nightfighter and two fighter training *Geschwader*. Altogether, it is estimated that the defenders flew some 800 individual sorties, and the Luftwaffe did not just have numbers on its side (nearly four fighters for every bomber that made it through to the target area). Its controllers were by now well versed in the enemy's tactics and limitations too.

The first *Jagdgruppen* to be scrambled were therefore held in check to the east of Aachen, just beyond the range of the bombers' escorting Thunderbolts. Once these USAAF fighters showed signs of turning back, the slaughter could begin.

The 'local' Fw 190 *Gruppen* again led the attack. In little more than 15 minutes, and at a cost of only two pilots wounded, I. and II./JG 1 claimed seven B-17s downed and eight *Herausschüsse*. The first two fell to Hauptmann Schnoor, the *Kommandeur* of I./JG 1, and Oberleutnant Rudolf Engleder – their eighth and tenth heavy bomber victories respectively. Engleder would also be credited with one of the *Herausschüsse* in a second pass only minutes later, while another provided the first heavy bomber success for future Knight's Cross recipient Oberfeldwebel Leo Schuhmacher of 6./JG 1. This was actually Schuhmacher's fifth victory of the war to date, the first four having been scored when he was a *Zerstörer* pilot back in 1940.

Meanwhile, I. and II./JG 26 were claiming a more modest five Flying Fortresses destroyed and two *Herausschüsse*. Again, one of the first to go down was credited to a *Gruppenkommandeur*, Major Johannes Seifert of II/.JG 26, while the *Kapitän* of his 7. *Staffel*, Hauptmann Johannes Naumann – who rejoiced in the nickname of 'Focke' – took his heavy bomber score to five. Oberfeldwebel Adolf 'Addi' Glunz of 5. *Staffel* had the distinction of despatching the only P-47 Thunderbolt lost on this day.

After running the gauntlet of Focke-Wulfs over the Dutch-German border areas, the remaining bombers battled on to Schweinfurt, where they inflicted major damage on the town's ball-bearing factories. Luftwaffe fighters kept up their attacks as the B-17s then turned and headed for home. Nor did the bomber crews gain their hoped for respite at the German frontier. The P-47s and Spitfires that were scheduled to escort them back to the Channel coast had been unable to take off from their cloud-covered UK bases.

Fortunately for the bombers, the same bad weather front stretched into the Continent, preventing those Luftwaffe fighters that had returned to their airfields in the Low Countries from scrambling for a second sortie. It also covered much of northeast France, hampering the efforts of Major Egon Mayer's JG 2 to deliver one last telling blow against the Schweinfurt force. Nonetheless, the Fw 190 pilots of I. and III./JG 2 were credited with eight more of the B-17s before the last of them headed out over the Channel towards the safety of southern England. One of the claimants was 12./JG 2's Oberleutnant Herbert Huppertz, whose Flying Fortress went down to the southeast of Verdun. Although Huppertz had already accounted for four earlier B-17s engaged in operations over France, this is believed to have been his first Defence of the Reich success.

The Luftwaffe units involved in the 14 October operation claimed a staggering 148 enemy aircraft destroyed. Although the Eighth's true losses were less than half that figure (60 bombers, plus 'Addi' Glunz's Thunderbolt), 'Second Schweinfurt' represented a decisive tactical victory for the defenders. It also signalled the end for the concept of unescorted daylight bombing. There would be 16 more incursions into German airspace before the close of 1943, but all would be shallow-penetration raids mounted against the northern and western peripheries of the Reich. None would venture beyond the range of available fighter cover. 'Second Schweinfurt' was one more turning point in the Defence of the Reich campaign. To borrow a well-known saying, it might not have been the beginning of the end, but it *was* the end of the beginning.

After the mayhem of Schweinfurt there was only one mission over Germany during the latter half of October. The target for the operation of 20 October was the small town of Düren, just to the east of Aachen – the very area where the Luftwaffe's fighters had gathered while waiting for the P-47s to turn back six days earlier. Heavy cloud affected both attackers and defenders alike, and only three bombers were claimed by Fw 190s. The first was the *Herausschuss* credited to Oberstleutnant Josef

Oberfeldwebel Leo Schuhmacher of 6./JG 1 studies the defensive armament on a model B-17. He would put theory to the test during 'Second Schweinfurt' on 14 October 1943, claiming a Flying Fortress *Herausschuss* on that date as the first of his seven Defence of the Reich heavy bomber successes

Enjoying what is clearly a toothsome snack, Oberleutnant Herbert Huppertz, the *Staffelkapitän* of 12./JG 2, was another who opened his Defence of the Reich bomber score sheet during 'Second Schweinfurt'. His tally had risen to ten by the time he too fell victim to US fighters over Normandy

Priller, the *Kommodore* of JG 26, shortly after the B-17s had crossed the French coast north of the Somme estuary. Another was the solitary bomber from the 390th BG chanced upon and downed by 6./JG 1's Unteroffizier Zinkl near the Dutch town of Hertogenbosch some 30 minutes later. His Fw 190 was hit by return fire from the Flying Fortress and Zinkl was forced to bail out. His fighter was JG 1's only combat loss of the day.

JG 26's casualties included four Fw 190 pilots killed, at least two of whom fell to P-47s. It was a portent of things to come.

The Defence of the Reich arena was becoming a different battlefield altogether. The presence of US escort fighters (henceforth in ever-increasing numbers) meant that Luftwaffe pilots no longer enjoyed the luxury of being able to formate unmolested beyond the range of the bombers' defensive fire and then decide when, where and how to deliver their attack. Protected by their own fighters, the bombers would be harder to approach. Kills would become more difficult to achieve and losses would inevitably begin to escalate.

That sombre scenario still lay some way in the future, however. The target for the Eighth's mission of 3 November – the heaviest yet with more than 500 bombers taking part – was a familiar one: Wilhelmshaven. The only Focke-Wulf *Gruppen* to engage were I. and II./JG 1, up from Deelen and Rheine, respectively. They claimed just three B-17s between them, and lost a pilot each. 1. *Staffel's* Feldwebel Johannes Rathenow was killed south of Wilhelmshaven in an encounter with the bombers and a group of their escorting P-38s (the Lightnings were flying only their second mission over Germany). As an unteroffizier serving with the Bf 109-equipped 10./JG 1, it was Rathenow who had shot down the RAF Boston during the Eighth Air Force's first ever mission on

Groundcrew push Oberstleutnant Josef Priller's machine back into the cover of a hedgerow. Typical of the aircraft flown by the *Kommodore* of JG 26, it carries both his 'lucky' number 13 and his personal emblem – the ace-of-hearts playing card bearing the name *'Jutta'*. The unmistakable figure of 'Pips' Priller himself can be seen in the background immediately below the port mainwheel leg radius rod

The growing numbers of US escort fighters inevitably led to increasing losses among the Luftwaffe's *Jagdgruppen*. The pilot of this unidentified Fw 190 jettisons his cockpit canopy and (presumably) bails out before his machine hits the ground and explodes

The Fw 190 *Gruppen* also suffered their fair share of accidents. I./JG 1's 'White 4' came to grief at Schiphol some time in the late summer of 1943

Independence Day, 4 July 1942. Since that time, having converted to Fw 190s, he had claimed five Flying Fortresses on Defence of the Reich operations, the last of them downed during 'Second Schweinfurt'. The Wilhelmshaven mission had cost the Americans seven B-17s in all. They lost another eight two days later during the 5 November attack on Gelsenkirchen, together with three B-24s (*text continues on page 46*)

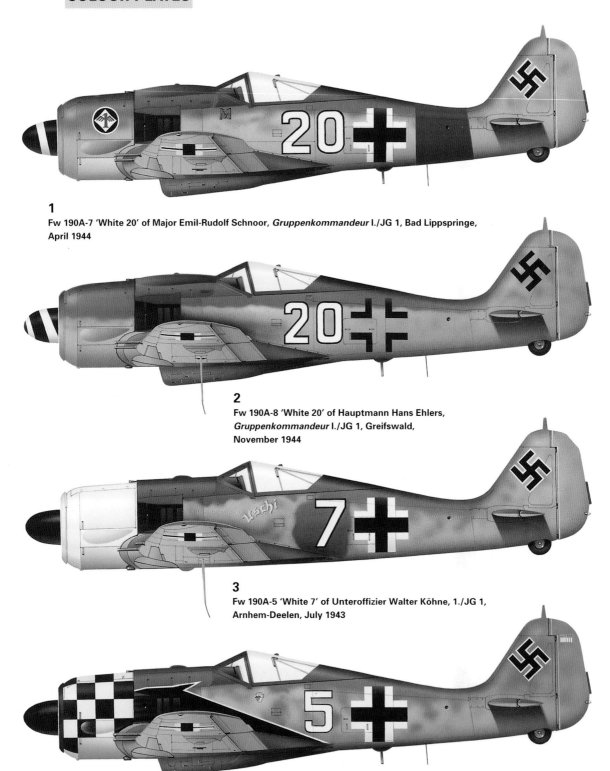

1
Fw 190A-7 'White 20' of Major Emil-Rudolf Schnoor, *Gruppenkommandeur* I./JG 1, Bad Lippspringe, April 1944

2
Fw 190A-8 'White 20' of Hauptmann Hans Ehlers, *Gruppenkommandeur* I./JG 1, Greifswald, November 1944

3
Fw 190A-5 'White 7' of Unteroffizier Walter Köhne, 1./JG 1, Arnhem-Deelen, July 1943

4
Fw 190A-6 'White 5' of Unteroffizier Rudolf Hübl, 1./JG 1, Arnhem-Deelen, December 1943

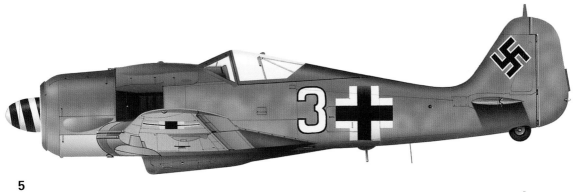

5
Fw 190A-8 'White 3' of Leutnant Anton-Rudolf Piffer, *Staffelkapitän* 1./JG 1, Le Mans, June 1944

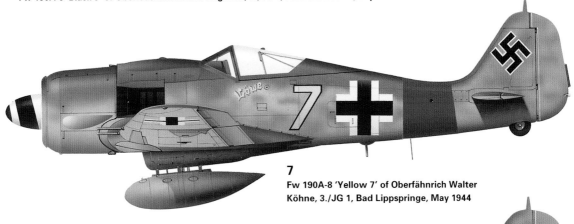

6
Fw 190A-6 'Black 3' of Oberleutnant Rudolf Engleder, 2./JG 1, Arnhem-Deelen, September 1943

7
Fw 190A-8 'Yellow 7' of Oberfähnrich Walter Köhne, 3./JG 1, Bad Lippspringe, May 1944

8
Fw 190A-7 'Red 22' of Oberfeldwebel Leo Schuhmacher, *Gruppenstab II.*/JG 1, Störmede, April 1944

9
Fw 190A-5 'Yellow 12' of Oberleutnant Harry Koch, *Staffelkapitän* 6./JG 1,
Woensdrecht, April 1943

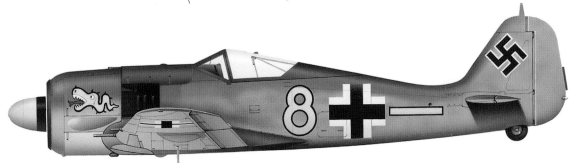

10
Fw 190A-4 'Yellow 8' of Oberfeldwebel Leo Schuhmacher, 6./JG 1,
Rheine, July 1943

11
Fw 190A-7 'Yellow 7' of Major Heinz Bär, 6./JG 1,
Rheine, January 1944

12
Fw 190A-4 'Yellow 12' of Unteroffizier Hans-Georg
Güthenke, 9./JG 1, Husum, March 1943

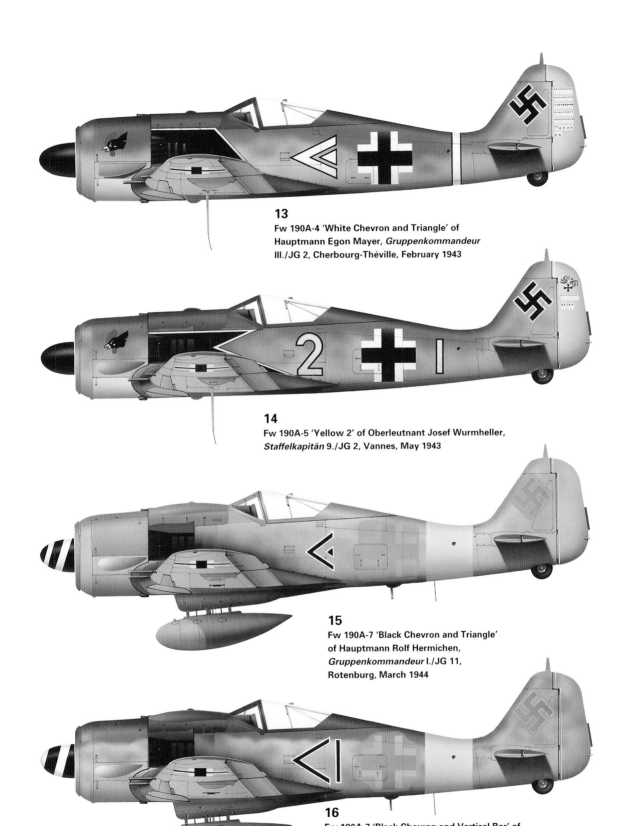

13
Fw 190A-4 'White Chevron and Triangle' of
Hauptmann Egon Mayer, *Gruppenkommandeur*
III./JG 2, Cherbourg-Théville, February 1943

14
Fw 190A-5 'Yellow 2' of Oberleutnant Josef Wurmheller,
Staffelkapitän 9./JG 2, Vannes, May 1943

15
Fw 190A-7 'Black Chevron and Triangle'
of Hauptmann Rolf Hermichen,
Gruppenkommandeur I./JG 11,
Rotenburg, March 1944

16
Fw 190A-7 'Black Chevron and Vertical Bar' of
Leutnant Hans Schrangl, *Gruppen-Adjutant* I./JG 11,
Rotenburg, March 1944

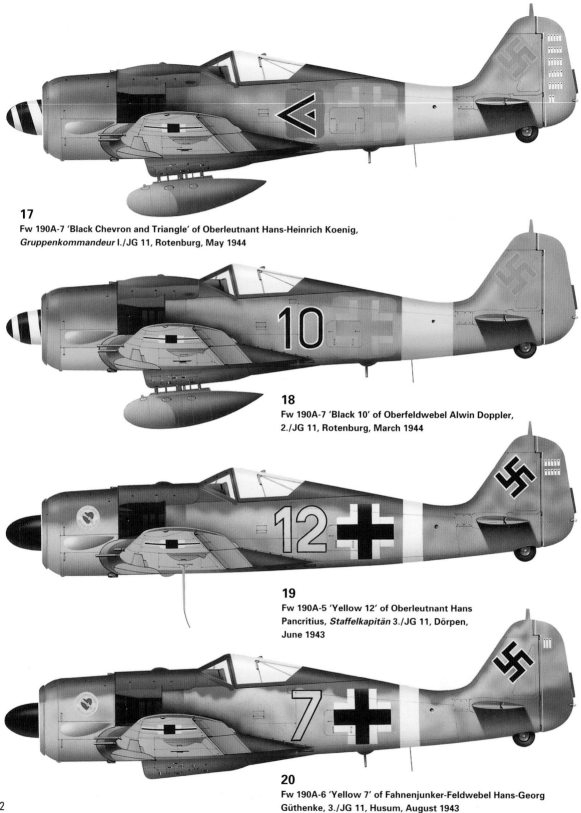

17
Fw 190A-7 'Black Chevron and Triangle' of Oberleutnant Hans-Heinrich Koenig, *Gruppenkommandeur* I./JG 11, Rotenburg, May 1944

18
Fw 190A-7 'Black 10' of Oberfeldwebel Alwin Doppler, 2./JG 11, Rotenburg, March 1944

19
Fw 190A-5 'Yellow 12' of Oberleutnant Hans Pancritius, *Staffelkapitän* 3./JG 11, Dörpen, June 1943

20
Fw 190A-6 'Yellow 7' of Fahnenjunker-Feldwebel Hans-Georg Güthenke, 3./JG 11, Husum, August 1943

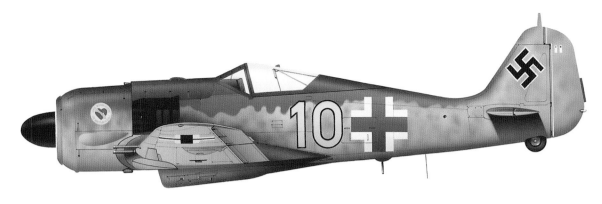

21
Fw 190A-6 'Yellow 10' of Feldwebel Heinz Stöwer, 3./JG 11, Husum, September 1943

22
Fw 190A-7 'Yellow 12' of Leutnant Hans-Georg Güthenke, 3./JG 11, Rotenburg, May 1944

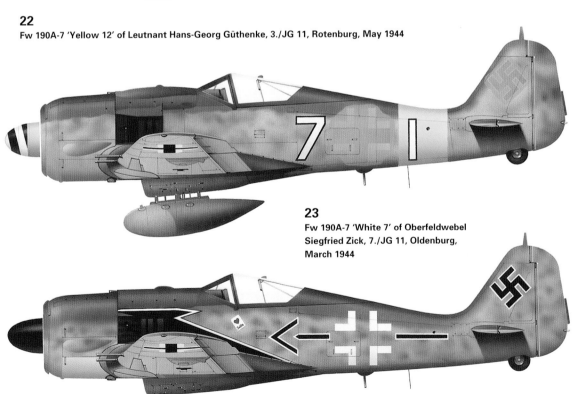

23
Fw 190A-7 'White 7' of Oberfeldwebel
Siegfried Zick, 7./JG 11, Oldenburg,
March 1944

24
Fw 190A-6 'Black Chevron and Horizontal Bars' of Oberstleutnant Josef Priller, *Geschwaderkommodore* JG 26,
St Omer-Wizernes, February 1944

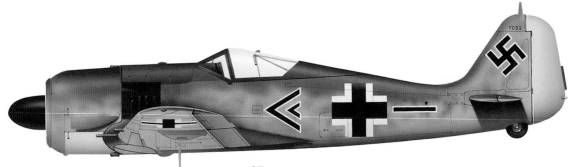

25
Fw 190A-4 'Black Double Chevron' of Hauptmann
Wilhelm-Ferdinand Galland, *Gruppenkommandeur*
II./JG 26, Volkel, August 1943

26
Fw 190A-7 'White 5' of Oberleutnant Walter Matoni,
Staffelkapitän 5./JG 26, Cambrai-Süd, March 1944

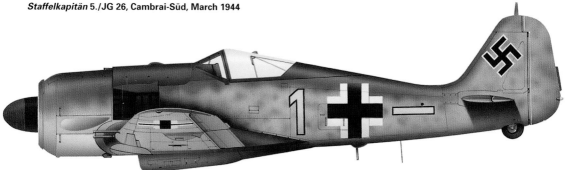

27
Fw 190A-6 'Yellow 1' of Hauptmann Hans Naumann, *Staffelkapitän* 6./JG 26,
Vitry-en-Artois, July 1943

28
Fw 190A-8 'Black 9' of Leutnant Adolf Glunz, *Staffelkapitän* 6./JG 26,
Guyancourt, June 1944

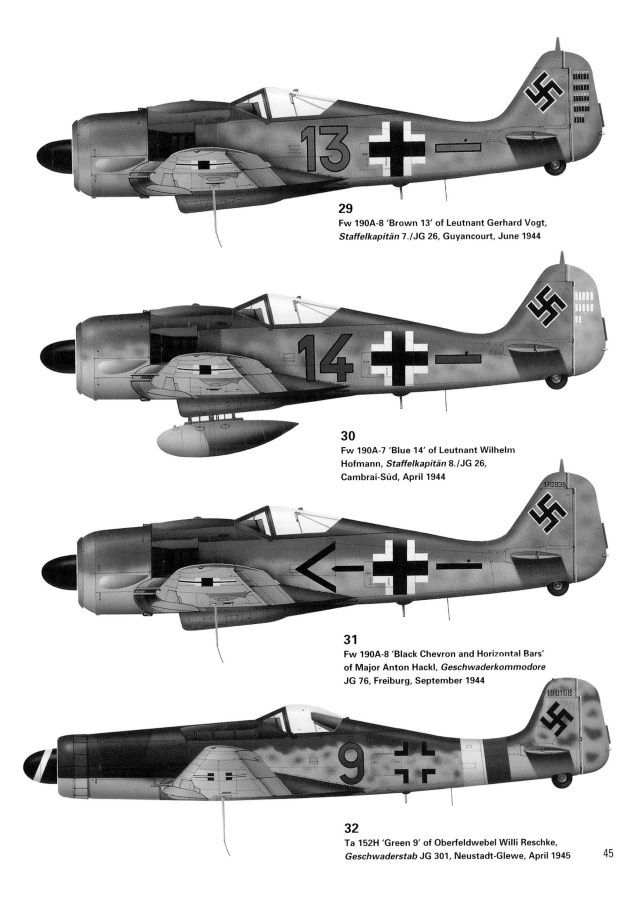

29
Fw 190A-8 'Brown 13' of Leutnant Gerhard Vogt,
Staffelkapitän 7./JG 26, Guyancourt, June 1944

30
Fw 190A-7 'Blue 14' of Leutnant Wilhelm
Hofmann, *Staffelkapitän* 8./JG 26,
Cambrai-Süd, April 1944

31
Fw 190A-8 'Black Chevron and Horizontal Bars'
of Major Anton Hackl, *Geschwaderkommodore*
JG 76, Freiburg, September 1944

32
Ta 152H 'Green 9' of Oberfeldwebel Willi Reschke,
Geschwaderstab JG 301, Neustadt-Glewe, April 1945

from the Liberator force carrying out a simultaneous strike against Münster. Among the 13 Luftwaffe *Gruppen* sent up in response to these two raids were the Focke-Wulfs of I. and II./JG 1, I./JG 11 and I./JG 26.

Faced with determined US fighter opposition, the four *Gruppen* managed to claim just six bombers for the loss of two pilots – both from 3./JG 1 – killed in action near Düsseldorf. Among the claimants was future *Viermot* ace Unteroffizier Walter Köhne, also of 3./JG 1, who was credited with a B-17 *Herausschuss* over the Dutch coast, but whose P-47 was disallowed for lack of witnesses. The recently appointed *Gruppenkommandeur* of I./JG 11, Hauptmann Rolf Hermichen, who had previously served as the *Staffelkapitän* of 3./JG 26, claimed an identical duo. His kills were both confirmed, however.

The Eighth planned another double raid for 11 November, this time with attacks to be made on Wesel and Münster. Once again the weather dictated otherwise. Despite the use of radar-equipped B-17 pathfinders, all nine groups of the Wesel force had to turn back. The conditions also hindered the defenders' response, with only six of the nine *Jagdgruppen* scrambled making contact with the enemy. The three Fw 190 *Gruppen* that did so claimed a total of nine B-17s, plus four of their escorting fighters. Although one of the two bombers downed by 5./JG 26's 'Addi' Glunz southeast of Rotterdam was subsequently disallowed, the other sufficed to take his Defence of the Reich bomber score to five.

Among the JG 1 claimants adding to their *Viermot* scores were Hauptmann Schnoor, who got one, and 2. *Staffel's* Oberfeldwebel Anton-Rudolf Piffer, whose brace of *Herausschüsse* took his tally to ten. Piffer's *Staffelkapitän*, Oberleutnant Rudolf Engleder, was credited with a P-38, although the only US fighters reportedly lost on this date were three P-47s.

The number of fighters that the Eighth Air Force was putting into the air to escort and support its heavy bombers was growing at a rate that was alarming to the Germans. The eight groups despatched on 11 November totalled more than 400 machines in all. Before the year was out that figure would have risen to 500+. Already overstretched on every fighting front, the Luftwaffe fighter arm was utterly unable to keep pace with such growth. Very few new *Jagdgeschwader* were being formed, with the Luftwaffe's preferred method of adding to its numbers being to increase the size of its existing *Jagdgruppen* from three *Staffeln* to four. The two westernmost *Jagdgeschwader*, JGs 2 and 26, had already undergone this transition. JGs 1 and 11 would follow suit in August 1944.

The composition of many *Jagdgeschwader* – specifically those operating a mix of both Bf 109s and Fw 190s – also enabled a division of responsibilities to be made. This was intended to increase their effectiveness, with those *Gruppen* equipped with Bf 109s being employed primarily to keep the

'Fips' Philipp's replacement as *Geschwaderkommodore* of JG 1 was the highly experienced Oberst Walter Oesau, who is seen here (centre) in the company of the Inspector General of the Luftwaffe *Generalfeldmarschall* Erhard Milch (right)

enemy's escorting fighters occupied, thereby allowing those flying the Fw 190, an altogether more robust machine and much steadier gun platform, a better chance of getting at the bombers.

One last measure taken was the transfer from other theatres back into the Reich of successful, high scoring pilots – especially accomplished unit leaders – whose experience, it was felt, would prove invaluable in what was rapidly becoming the most critical campaign of the European air war.

One such pilot, 202-victory Major Hermann Graf, had already been recalled from the eastern front to establish a special high-altitude Bf 109 *Gruppe*. Since the loss of Hans Philipp, he had also been serving as acting-*Kommodore* of JG 1, before being appointed *Geschwaderkommodore* of JG 11 on 11 November. Philipp's official replacement as leader of JG 1 was Oberst Walter Oesau, who took office on 12 November. Wearing the Oak Leaves with Swords, Oesau had been the *Kommodore* of JG 2 in northern France since the summer of 1941, but had spent the last four months as the *Jafü Bretagne* (OC Fighters Brittany).

The various organisational and other changes made within the Defence of the Reich command, including those outlined above, did not take place overnight of course. And for the remainder of November 1943 at least it was still very much business as usual for the Fw 190 *Gruppen*. The Eighth's next three incursions, all flown against Bremen, cost the Americans a total of 54 heavy bombers, exactly half of which were claimed by the Focke-Wulfs of JGs 1 and 11.

The B-24 groups suffered the bulk of the casualties sustained during the Bremen raid of 13 November. They were first intercepted over Schleswig-Holstein by Hauptmann Rolf Hermichen's I./JG 11. One of the eight Liberators downed was credited to the *Gruppenkommandeur*.

More top brass in the form of Generaloberst Jürgen Stumpff (second from left), newly-appointed GOC *Luftwaffenbefehlshaber Mitte*, who is seen here on a visit of inspection to I./JG 11's Husum base in late 1943. He is being saluted by Oberleutnant Hans-Heinrich Koenig, the *Staffelkapitän* of 3./JG 11. Like Günther Specht, 'King' Koenig had also lost an eye in combat earlier in the war. This did not prevent him from eventually returning to operational flying. Indeed, he became the fifth-ranking Fw 190 Defence of the Reich anti-bomber ace with a final total of 19 victories

Another provided the first Fw 190 heavy bomber victory for Oberleutnant Hans-Heinrich Koenig of 3. *Staffel*. 'King' Koenig's first four kills had been achieved against the RAF as a *Zerstörer* and nightfighter pilot early in the war. Despite being wounded in 1942 and losing the sight of one eye, he had since returned to operations and would quickly rise to become one of the Defence of the Reich's foremost anti-bomber *Experten*.

When the Eighth returned to Bremen on 26 November it was the Flying Fortresses that were to feel the weight of the Luftwaffe's fighter attacks – indeed, only one of that day's string of Focke-Wulf claims was for a Liberator. A B-17 downed southwest of the target area was heavy bomber number five for Hauptmann Walter Hoeckner, the *Gruppenkommandeur* of II./JG 1. A second pilot to achieve *Viermot* acedom on this date was 4./JG 1's Oberfeldwebel Detlef Lüth.

The three Fw 190 *Gruppen* of JGs 1 and 11 submitted claims for only six B-17s during the Eighth's third and final visit of the month to Bremen on 29 November. Of these, one went to Walter Hoeckner, another made a heavy bomber ace out of Leutnant Hans Ehlers, the *Staffelkapitän* of 3./JG 1, while a third provided fellow-*Staffelkapitän* Oberleutnant Alfred Grislawski of 1./JG 1 with his first Focke-Wulf Defence of the Reich bomber success. The latter Flying Fortress was, in fact, the Knight's Cross-wearing Grislawski's 114th victory of the war to date. He had been a member of Hermann Graf's legendary 9./JG 52 on the eastern front (where he had amassed a score of 109) and was one of the group of pilots that Graf had brought back with him when he was recalled to the Reich.

Although seriously impaired by the weather, the Eighth's planned attack on Solingen, in the Rhineland, on 30 November was undeniably another portent of things to come for the defending Focke-Wulfs. Only I. and II./JG 1 made contact with the enemy. I. *Gruppe* became embroiled with P-47s shortly after taking off from their Deelen base and lost two pilots killed. II. *Gruppe* sighted a formation of B-17s to the southwest of Krefeld but its pilots were unable to break through the screen of escorting fighters, which outnumbered their Fw 190s by more than twelve-to-one.

The Luftwaffe had more success when the bombers returned to Solingen 24 hours later. This time, for the loss of just one of their number, the Focke-Wulfs of I. and II./JG 1 and I./JG 11 claimed a total of ten heavy bombers. JG 1 *Staffelkapitäne* Alfred Grislawski and Harry Koch got a pair of Flying Fortresses apiece, while Rolf Hermichen of I./JG 11 was credited with a brace of Liberators (one an *Herausschuss*). Single B-17s went to Hans Ehlers and Rudolf Engleder, their sixth and thirteenth 'heavies' respectively.

JGs 2 and 26 were also involved in the action on this 1 December. Three of I./JG 26's five claimants for heavy bombers were *Staffelkapitäne*, with Oberleutnant Artur Beese of 1./JG 26 accounting for his third (his opening pair had gone down during 'First Schweinfurt'), 2./JG 26's Leutnant Karl Willius gaining his first and Oberleutnant Wolfgang Neu of 4./JG 26 claiming his second. Another omen of what lay ahead for the Reich's defenders was that all three would be killed in action before the end of spring 1944, as too would Oberstleutnant Egon Mayer,

Drab but deadly. These early P-51B Mustangs of the Ninth Air Force's 354th FG were harbingers of hard times ahead for the Luftwaffe's Focke-Wulf *Jagdgruppen*

the *Geschwaderkommodore* of JG 2. He had taken his Defence of the Reich heavy bomber tally to five on this day.

The most ominous sign of all went seemingly unnoticed and unreported midway through the next ten days of persistent rain and cloud that prevented the enemy from making a single foray into Germany. On 5 December 1943 the Eighth's bombers attacked targets in western France. Among the nine groups of escorting fighters was one borrowed from the Ninth Air Force. It was equipped with the P-51B Mustang, and this really *did* signify the beginning of the end.

That end was still some way off, but the scales were now tipped firmly in favour of the Americans – although it might have been hard to convince the crews of the 104 bombers still to be lost in the final six raids of 1943 of that fact. For the first four of those raids the Eighth returned to its familiar haunts in the north. The 11 December mission against Emden included the 'borrowed' P-51Bs as part of its fighter escort. It was the first time that the Mustang had entered Reich airspace.

Among the eight Luftwaffe *Gruppen* sent up in response to the bombers were the three Fw 190 units of JGs 1 and 11. Between them they were credited with a total of ten B-17s and a single B-24. Unit leaders were again prominent among the claimants, with Rudolf Engleder (I./JG 1), Hans Ehlers (3./JG 1), Harry Koch (6./JG 1), Rolf Hermichen (I./JG 11) and Hans-Heinrich Koenig (3./JG 11) each getting a Flying Fortress. 'King' Koenig, however, had to bail out wounded after despatching his second B-17 of the campaign west of the target area.

Two days later, on 13 December, a maximum effort by the enemy against ports in northern Germany marked another milestone in (or yet another nail in the coffin of?) the Defence of the Reich campaign. For the first time the Eighth sent more than 1000 aircraft – bombers *and* fighters – on a mission against Germany. Due to the severe weather over the Continent, very few Luftwaffe machines rose to meet them. II./JG 1 at Rheine managed to scramble just seven Focke-Wulfs in response, but to little purpose. The only claims (for two B-17s and a single B-24) came from three nightfighter crews of NJG 3, whose blind-flying experience made them far better able to cope with the conditions.

On 16 December Bremen, which had been one of the targets attacked three days earlier, was visited again. The weather had improved only marginally in the interim, but did allow elements of I. and II./JG 1 to take off. The latter's five Focke-Wulfs sighted a formation of some 250-300 bombers, but were kept at bay by about 40 of the enemy's fighter escort. This meant that the day's 11 victories were all claimed by pilots of I. *Gruppe*.

Hauptmann Alfred Grislawski and Oberleutnant Hans Ehlers, the *Kapitäne* of 1. and 3. *Staffeln* respectively, each added a Flying Fortress to their scores. The B-17 *Herausschuss* credited to 2./JG 1's Feldwebel Walter Köhne took his tally to five, thereby making him a heavy bomber ace. Two other members of 2. *Staffel*, Oberfeldwebel Anton-Rudolf Piffer and the *Kapitän*, Oberleutnant Rudolf Engleder, claimed a brace of Flying Fortresses apiece. However, while attacking his second victim head-on, Engleder's armoured windscreen was hit by return fire and he was wounded in the face by splinters. Unable to see, he was guided to nearby Twente airfield by 'Toni' Piffer, who then talked him down into a blind landing over the R/T. Rudolf Engleder would spend the next two months in hospital, but regained the sight in both eyes.

20 December saw the Eighth Air Force's bombers return to Bremen for the third time in little more than a week. With I./JG 11 stood down, the only Fw 190 opposition they faced came from I. and II./JG 1. The two *Gruppen* claimed a total of six B-17s. Five of the Flying Fortresses were added to the score sheets of pilots who were already *Viermot* aces. The sixth raised Hauptmann Alfred Grislawski to similar status by providing him with his fifth bomber kill since being appointed *Staffelkapitän* of 1./JG 1.

Alfred Grislawski claimed another B-17 48 hours later during the Eighth's double strike against Osnabrück and Münster on 22 December. Once again, I. and II./JG 1 were the only Fw 190 units among the 11 Luftwaffe *Gruppen* sent up to engage the enemy. The Focke-Wulfs were credited with just three bombers (plus a P-38 for 'Toni' Piffer), but the day was overshadowed by the loss of Hauptmann Harry Koch, the popular and long-serving *Staffelkapitän* of 6./JG 1, who lost his life in a mid-air collision with his wingman north of Osnabrück.

Despite the worsening winter weather, 2./JG 1's 'Black 3' taxies out at Dortmund to take off. The black-and-white striped cowling stands out clearly. What is less obvious is the fact that the aircraft's individual numeral '3' is thinly outlined in red, and that the dark patch aft of the fuselage *Balkenkreuz* is JG 1's newly introduced red Defence of the Reich recognition band

Having previously flown with JG 26, the then Oberleutnant Koch had been a founder member of the Bf 109-equipped III./JG 1, becoming the *Kapitän* of that *Gruppe's* 7. *Staffel* upon its activation in February 1942. Since taking over 6./JG 1 in March 1943, he had added a further 17 victories to his previous 13 kills. All but four of his later successes had been US heavy bombers. He was also credited with two 'final destructions' which, although they had earned him a point apiece, were not classed as victories by JG 1. This was contrary to some other *Jagdgeschwader*, which apparently regarded them as such – another prime example of that old adage so often quoted by Germany's wartime pilots, 'The only hard and fast rule in the Luftwaffe was that there were no hard and fast rules!'.

Hauptmann Harry Koch had been awarded the German Cross in Gold on 17 October 1943, but many were of the opinion that his final score of 30 enemy aircraft destroyed fully merited the Knight's Cross. One of the unavoidable anomalies of the Luftwaffe's awards system was that the astronomical scores currently being amassed by fighter pilots on the eastern front had raised the criteria for decorations to such high levels that not one of the pioneering Defence of the Reich aces was honoured with the Knight's Cross.

The Eighth's final incursion into Reich airspace in 1943 was the 30 December raid on Ludwigshafen, which involved a combined force of very nearly 1300 bombers and fighters. In order to avoid the Luftwaffe defences along the North Sea coast, the Americans' approach route to the target took them over France – a classic case of out of the frying-pan

The snow lies thicker on Dortmund's runway as I./JG 1 prepares for a massed take-off. Like 'Black 3' seen in the previous photograph, these machines are also fitted with ventral fuel tanks and are wearing red aft fuselage bands

As the leader runs up his engine, the aircraft immediately behind him are almost completely hidden by the flying snow

Although the B-24 that Oberleutnant Walter Matoni of 6./JG 26 claimed on 30 December 1943 came down in northern France, it was en route to Ludwigshafen, in Germany, and thus provided him with the first of his 10+ Defence of the Reich heavy bomber victories

into the fire, for their course placed them within easy range of the two veteran western-based *Jagdgeschwader*, JGs 2 and 26. Over half of the 23 bombers lost fell victim to fighters, with seven being claimed by the Focke-Wulfs of I. and II./JG 26.

Three of the claimants were future *Viermot* aces and Knight's Cross recipients. The Flying Fortress downed near Soissons by Leutnant Karl 'Charly' Willius, the *Staffelkapitän* of 2./JG 26, was his second. A Liberator lost in the same area was the first Defence of the Reich victory for 6. *Staffel's* Oberleutnant Walter Matoni, while another B-17 shot down closer to the French coast as the attackers were retiring provided a fifth for Leutnant Waldemar 'Waldi' Radener of 7./JG 26.

So ended 1943, and the first half of 1944 would only bring more of the same. With the Eighth's strength increasing all the while – not least with the entry into service of its own P-51 Mustangs – the next stage of the daylight offensive would be dominated by the ferocious air battles fought during February's so-called 'Big Week', the first attack on Berlin in March and the start of the campaign against the Reich's oil industry in May.

'BIG WEEK', BERLIN AND OIL

The primary target for the first raid on the Reich in 1944 was once again Kiel. The mission of 4 January produced only one recorded claim by an Fw 190 pilot – the *Herausschuss* of a Flying Fortress by 6./JG 1's Feldwebel Heinz Fuchs. A second strike against the same objective 24 hours later resulted in a trio of Liberators being credited to I./JG 11, one of them being the fifth heavy bomber for 2. *Staffel's* Unteroffizier Franz Steiner. Another B-24 gave Oberstleutnant Walter Oesau his 106th victory of the war and first Defence of the Reich heavy bomber kill since being appointed *Geschwaderkommodore* of JG 1.

The New Year brought little improvement in the weather. Pictured in the previous chapter taxiing out to take off, 'Black 3' of 2./JG 1 now gets a rudimentary wash down as a groundcrewman throws a bucket of dirty water over that red aft fuselage band. Note that the *Geschwader's* new 'Winged 1' unit badge is carried on the *left* side of the engine cowling only

The 'Winged 1', introduced by *Kommodore* Walter Oesau, is also clearly visible on the hinged cowling panel of this machine undergoing engine maintenance

Meanwhile, a smaller force of B-17s attacking targets of opportunity in the Düsseldorf area enabled I./JG 1 to claim five bombers. Leutnant Hans Ehlers, the *Staffelkapitän* of 3./JG 1, and 2. *Staffel's* Oberfeldwebel Anton-Rudolf Piffer got one apiece, taking their respective heavy bomber scores to 10 and 15. Unteroffizier Rudolf Hübl added another pair of *Herausschüsse* to the two he had claimed back in October to raise his overall tally to six.

On 7 January it was the turn of II./JG 26 to submit claims for three bombers. Although the *Gruppe* was based in France and all three of its victims were shot down over that country, the trio of B-17s had been part of a large formation returning from a second raid on Ludwigshafen. The highest scorer on that 7 January, however, was undoubtedly Oberstleutnant Egon Mayer, the *Geschwaderkommodore* of JG 2, who accounted for no fewer than four bombers (three B-24s and a B-17) in the Orléans area, thereby taking

The melting snow has now turned
to slush on the apron outside one
of I./JG 1's hangars at Dortmund
in January 1944

his final Defence of the Reich heavy bomber score to nine. In the same action Herbert Huppertz, now of 11./JG 2, downed a brace of Liberators to raise his total to six.

On 11 January the first major clash of the year took place between the Eighth Air Force and the Luftwaffe. The Americans put more than 650 bombers into the air, their primary targets being the aircraft factories at Brunswick, Oschersleben and Halberstadt. Confusing weather reports apparently caused the recall of most of the main Brunswick force, which attacked various targets of opportunity during its return flight, losing 18 of its number in the process. This left the 260+ B-17s of the Oschersleben and Halberstadt formations to face the full weight of the Luftwaffe's defences, which comprised 14 *Jagd-* and four *Zerstörergruppen*, plus elements from five *Nachtjagdgeschwader* and several other smaller units – little wonder that the Flying Fortress crews described it as the 'heaviest opposition encountered since "Second Schweinfurt".' In fact, the total of 60 bombers in all that failed to return on this date matched exactly the losses suffered on each of the historic Schweinfurt raids of 1943.

Another disturbing echo of Schweinfurt was that the P-47s of the fighter escort were unable to accompany the bombers all the way to the target area. During the most critical phase of the mission the B-17s' sole protection – apart from their own weapons – was provided by 44 Mustangs of the 354th FG, which was still 'on loan' to VIII Fighter Command from the Ninth Air Force.

All three Fw 190 *Gruppen* of JGs 1 and 11 were involved in the day's action. As so often in the past, I./JG 1 was among the first units to engage the enemy. One of the five B-17s it claimed was the seventh Flying Fortress in a row to be credited to the *Kapitän* of 1. *Staffel*, Hauptmann Alfred Grislawski. Shortly afterwards, II./JG 1 encountered a formation of more than 50 unescorted B-17s. In the absence of enemy fighters, the *Gruppe* – led on this occasion by Leutnant Rüdiger Kirchmayr, the *Staffelkapitän* of 5./JG 1 – was able to carry out a series of three coordinated attacks, claiming the destruction of nine bombers.

In the event, only two were subsequently confirmed. They were firsts for Kirchmayr and for Oberfeldwebel Leo Schuhmacher of 6. *Staffel*, although the latter had already been credited with an *Herausschuss* during 'Second Schweinfurt'. I./JG 11's two victories on this date went to NCO pilots of 2. *Staffel*, both of them established *Viermot* aces – Feldwebel Alwin Doppler getting his eighth, while Unteroffizier Franz Steiner's *Herausschuss* was his sixth. The day's total tally of nine heavy bombers had cost the three *Gruppen* just one pilot killed and one wounded.

The Focke-Wulfs had not finished with the Flying Fortresses yet, however. After a succession of running battles with other *Gruppen*, the bombers were intercepted by I. and II./JG 26 as they made their way back out over the Low Countries. Hauptmann Karl Borris' I. *Gruppe* was also fortunate enough to chance upon a small formation of some 20 unescorted B-17s. After delivering a concerted frontal assault, the German pilots regrouped and came in again from the rear. In a matter of minutes they too had claimed nine bombers and, unlike II./JG 1's earlier attacks, all but one of their claims were allowed. Among the eight successful pilots was 2./JG 26's Leutnant Karl Willius. It was his third heavy bomber victory of the Defence of the Reich campaign.

II./JG 26 attacked another group of bombers a few minutes later, but the *Gruppe* managed to down only one of them. This provided a second for 6. *Staffel's* Oberleutnant Walter Matoni. The *Gruppe* was, however, also credited with a *Herausschuss* and a 'final destruction'.

As a footnote to the day's events, it should perhaps be mentioned that amongst the aircraft lost was the first US heavy bomber to be shot down by a Focke-Wulf of *Sturmstaffel* 1, an experimental unit that had accompanied I./JG 1 into action. This *Staffel* was the forerunner of the specialised *Sturmgruppen*, whose heavily armed and armoured Fw 190s would be taking the leading role in Defence of the Reich anti-bomber operations in the not too distant future (for further details see *Osprey Aviation Elite Units 20 - Luftwaffe Sturmgruppen*).

A prolonged spell of bad weather meant that it would be two weeks before the Eighth next attempted to venture into Reich airspace. Even then, the 24 January raid on Frankfurt had to be recalled because of worsening conditions on the day. Only 50 of the leading Flying Fortresses that were already over the Belgian-German border opted to carry on, selecting the large power station at Eschweiler – just 12 miles inside Germany – as their nearest target of opportunity.

The adverse weather also restricted the Luftwaffe's response to the incoming bombers, but *Staffelkapitän* Alfred Grislawski of 1./JG 1 managed to down his eighth B-17 nevertheless, while one of his *Staffel* members, Rudolf Hübl, added yet another to his lengthening list of Flying Fortress *Herausschüsse* (his fifth in a row).

Although Leutnant Rüdiger Kirchmayr, the *Staffelkapitän* of 5./JG 1, did not claim his first Defence of the Reich heavy bomber until 11 January 1944, he had been a member of JG 1 for almost two years by then. He is seen here during his earlier service with 4. *Staffel* – hence the white *Tatzelwurm*

Another fledgling Fw 190 Defence of the Reich anti-bomber ace in early 1944 was Leutnant Wilhelm Hofmann, seen here in the cockpit of his 8./JG 26 machine. He was credited with his third B-17 during the Eighth's attack on Frankfurt on 29 January 1944

Photographed in one of those increasingly rare moments of relaxation, these two pilots of JG 1 accounted for four B-17s in the space of 20 minutes on 30 January. Oberleutnant Hans Ehlers (right), the *Kapitän* of 3. *Staffel*, claimed two of the Flying Fortresses, while his *Geschwaderkommodore*, Oberst Walter Oesau (left), had to be content with one bomber shot down and one 'final destruction'

Two pilots of II./JG 1 had already claimed a P-51 apiece over Belgium several minutes earlier. A number of the Ninth Air Force's Mustangs had been lost during the course of the preceding weeks, but most of them, it is believed, had been shot down by Bf 109s. If this pair *were* the two casualties admitted by the USAAF on this date, they could well be the first P-51s to fall victim to Defence of the Reich Fw 190s.

By 29 January the weather had cleared sufficiently to allow the Eighth to finally strike at Frankfurt. The attackers' route to and from the target area took them across northeast France and Belgium. This was territory zealously guarded by JG 26, and its two Fw 190 *Gruppen* were responsible for 21 of the 61 successes claimed by the defenders. No fewer than 18 *Gruppen* were hastily ordered to scramble in defence of Frankfurt – is it too fanciful to suppose that Göring did not want to risk another formal complaint from the local Gauleiter and a repetition of the carpeting he had received from Hitler following the previous raid on the city back in October?

Among the 16 heavy bomber claims submitted by I. and II./JG 26 were three *Herausschüsse* and one 'final destruction'. And among the claimants were Hauptmann Karl Borris, the *Kommandeur* of I. *Gruppe*, Oberleutnant Wolfgang Neu, the *Staffelkapitän* of 4./JG 26, 6. *Staffel's* Oberleutnant Walter Matoni and 8. *Staffel's* Leutnant Wilhelm Hofmann, each of whom added a third Flying Fortress to his personal Defence of the Reich heavy bomber tally.

Twenty-four hours later, when the Eighth struck at targets in the Brunswick and Hannover areas of northwest Germany, JG 26's Focke-Wulfs were able to down just three B-17s between them. The honours on this 30 January went instead to the Fw 190s of JG 1 with their 13 victories. *Geschwaderkommodore* Oberst Walter Oesau was credited with one Flying Fortress destroyed plus one 'final destruction'. Major Rudolf-Emil Schnoor, the *Kommandeur* of I. *Gruppe*, took his bomber score to ten, while the *Staffelkapitän* of 3./JG 1, Oberleutnant Hans Ehlers, claimed a brace of B-17s, thus boosting his growing tally of *Viermot* kills to a dozen.

During January III./JG 11 had been re-equipping with Fw 190s. The unit had taken delivery of its first Focke-Wulfs at the end of 1943, and conversion was then carried out on an individual *Staffel* basis while the *Gruppe* remained operational throughout. Hauptmann Anton Hackl's *Gruppenstab* had been the first to receive the new mounts. 7. and 8. *Staffeln* had reportedly completed conversion by the middle of the month, with 9. *Staffel* following suit shortly thereafter. From available references it would appear that four of the *Gruppe's* future *Viermot* aces, including the *Kommandeur* himself, had already added one or more heavy bombers to their scores before January was out.

The power of the press. The snow was still fairly thick on the ground at Cambrai-Epinoy in February 1944 when these pilots of II./JG 26 ambled out to their machines . . .

. . . but this was not dramatic enough for the visiting propaganda company photographer, who demanded that they put some life into it and enact an emergency scramble. Among those shown here complying with his wishes are Walter Matoni, in the lead wearing the peaked cap, and 'Addi' Glunz on the far left

The Eighth Air Force's first incursion into the Reich in February saw the bombers return to Wilhelmshaven and Emden, on the North Sea coast. The Fw 190s of JGs 1 and 11 were prevented from engaging the 'heavies' by the weather. This same 3 February was, however, noteworthy for the fact that it was the day on which the command responsible for the defence of the homeland, hitherto known as *Luftwaffenbefehlshaber Mitte* (literally 'Luftwaffe C-in-C Centre'), was officially redesignated to become the *Luftflotte Reich*.

Three of the enemy's next four raids on Germany were targeted at Frankfurt. That on 4 February was beset by poor weather, which

Using a fighter pilot's classic hand gestures, Oberleutnant Josef Wurmheller, the *Staffelkapitän* of 9./JG 2, describes his latest victory to fellow pilots. 'Sepp' Wurmheller's first Defence of the Reich heavy bomber was brought down near Le Tréport on 8 February 1944

hampered attackers and defenders alike. The only successful Fw 190 claimants for bombers on this date were four pilots of JG 26, each of whom already had several such victories to his name.

Four days later the *Geschwader* managed to bring down just one Flying Fortress (plus a 'final destruction'), while III./JG 2 was able to claim a pair. One of the latter, shot down near Le Tréport on the French Channel coast, was the first Defence of the Reich heavy bomber victory for the *Staffelkapitän* of 9./JG 2, Oberleutnant Josef Wurmheller. The Oak Leaves-wearing 'Sepp' Wurmheller had already accounted for no fewer than 15 Flying Fortresses engaged in attacking objectives in France. The most successful of the five Focke-Wulf *Gruppen* defending Frankfurt on 8 February had been I./JG 1, which was credited with five B-17s destroyed. Among the pilots adding further to their growing tallies of heavy bombers were Major Schnoor and Oberfeldwebel Piffer, who chalked up their 11th and 17th respectively.

On 10 February the Eighth turned its attention away from Frankfurt to strike at Brunswick. The change of target cost the Americans 29 of their heavy bombers. The Luftwaffe claimed 52, including three *Herausschüsse* and two 'final destructions' – 27 of the claims were submitted by the Fw 190 pilots of JGs 1 and 11. The JG 1 claimants included several already familiar names. *Geschwaderkommodore* Oberst Walter 'Gulle' Oesau was credited with his third, while 2. *Staffel's* Oberfeldwebel Erich Demuth joined the ranks of the aces by getting his fifth, as did 4. *Staffel's* Feldwebel Heinz Fuchs. Two other feldwebeln, Rudolf Hübl of 1./JG 1 and Walter Köhne of 3./JG 1, both took their scores to eight.

Among the six aviators from I./JG 11 credited with a B-17 on this date were two existing heavy bomber aces, Hauptmann Rolf Hermichen (eight kills) and Feldwebel Alwin Doppler (nine kills), two who were

Rotenburg, March 1944, and an obviously delighted Hauptmann Rolf Hermichen, *Gruppenkommandeur* of I./JG 11 (right), celebrates the news that he has been awarded the Knight's Cross. The three pilots congratulating him – all eventual Defence of the Reich anti-bomber aces – are, from the left, Oberfähnrich Gerhard Dreizehner (just visible in profile), Oberleutnant Hans-Heinrich Koenig and Leutnant Hans Schrangl

soon to achieve that status, Feldwebel Heinz Stöwer (four kills) and Oberleutnant Hans-Heinrich Koenig (three kills), and two whose Flying Fortresses were the first victories for both. Of the latter pair, Leutnant Hans Schrangl would go on to add ten further heavy bombers (and three fighters) to his score before being seriously injured in an emergency landing on 2 October, while Fahnenjunker-Feldwebel Gerhard Dreizehner would claim another four bombers (and a single P-47), all in the space of the next two months, before he was himself killed in action on 9 April.

III./JG 11's successes included a third Flying Fortress each for *Gruppenkommandeur* Hauptmann Anton 'Toni' Hackl and 7. *Staffel's* Oberfeldwebel Siegfried Zick.

Arguably the most famous name among the many claimants of 10 February was that of a certain major currently serving with 6./JG 1. It was decidedly unusual for someone with the rank of major to be flying as an ordinary *Staffel* member, but then Heinz 'Pritzl' Bär was no ordinary major. In fact, he was regarded by many as one of the Luftwaffe's ablest and most courageous fighter pilots. Claiming his first victory in the opening month of the war, he had subsequently risen to become the *Gruppenkommandeur* firstly of IV./JG 51 on the eastern front and then of I./JG 77 in North Africa.

Bär's success, the popularity he enjoyed among his peers and subordinates but, above all, his frank outspokenness had not endeared him to certain of his superiors, however. Official displeasure at his attitude reached right to the very top, to the Reichsmarschall himself. His posting away from I./JG 77 to the command of a fighter training unit could, perhaps, be looked upon as a legitimate use of his undoubted talents. Yet when, despite Bär's 179 victories and the Swords to the Oak Leaves that he wore around his neck, he was then transferred to the ranks of 6./JG 1 – even if nominally as a 'deputy *Staffelkapitän*' – it was demotion pure and simple.

JG 1's *Geschwaderkommodore* 'Gulle' Oesau, who was hewn from the same material as 'Pritzl' Bär, welcomed him with open arms. And it would not be long before the irrepressible Major Bär's roller-coaster operational career was on the way up again.

The Eighth Air Force's 11 February attack on Frankfurt cost it just five Flying Fortresses. The defending Focke-Wulfs claimed six. I./JG 11's sole victory was the second B-17 for Fahnenjunker-Feldwebel Dreizehner, while I. and II./JG 26's trio of kills included a fifth Defence of the Reich heavy bomber for 3. *Staffel's* Oberfeldwebel Erich Scheyda (the remaining pair of Flying Fortresses were credited to the *Sturmstaffel*). It was on this same 11 February that the first P-51 Mustang group to be assigned to the Eighth flew its maiden mission – a so-called 'milk run' escorting B-24s sent across the Channel to attack V-weapon sites in northern France.

For the next nine days the skies above the Reich remained quiet as the Eighth Air Force prepared itself

A respectful Major Heinz Bär (right) shakes the hand of his new *Geschwaderkommodore*, Oberst Walter Oesau

for Operation *Argument*, now better known simply as 'Big Week'. This planned series of daily, maximum effort missions was directly aimed at breaking the back of the Luftwaffe by destroying Germany's aircraft factories and annihilating its fighters in the air. Operation *Argument* was launched on Sunday, 20 February with the Eighth's first ever 1000-bomber raid. Supported by nearly 850 US fighters, it was targeted at a dozen aircraft manufacturing and assembly plants in more than five separate locations.

In all, the Eighth's 'Big Week' would actually consist of five operations spread over six days, on the last of which it was faced by no fewer than 36 Luftwaffe *Gruppen*. By its close the USAAF had lost 155 bombers, but the defending Luftwaffe units reported 250 fighters lost or written off and more than half that number damaged. The Eighth would fail in its stated aim of crippling Germany's aviation industry. Nor had the Luftwaffe been 'annihilated' in the air. Its losses had quickly been made good – at least numerically – and the *Luftflotte Reich* still remained a potent force (although the training of replacement pilots was no longer as thorough as it once had been).

There is one thing that 'Big Week' *did* accomplish, however, and that was to turn the tide of the campaign irrevocably against the Luftwaffe. In just over a year the Eighth had grown from less than 100 bombers, flying unescorted raids against single targets on the northernmost rim of Hitler's Reich, into a mighty armada of 1000 machines and more, supported and escorted by nearly as many fighters, striking simultaneously at various targets deep in central and eastern Germany. And as the Eighth's strength continued to increase – particularly in terms of its fighter force – so the Luftwaffe would find itself being swamped by sheer weight of numbers.

This process – which was, in effect, the penultimate phase of the Defence of the Reich campaign – began on the very first day of 'Big Week'. Although the Luftwaffe put elements of 26 *Gruppen* into the air, its controllers were confused by the multiplicity of targets and were unable to accurately forecast the enemy's intentions. As a result, relatively few engagements took place before the bombers reached their objectives, and even after the American formations had turned for home, the fighter attacks delivered by the Luftwaffe lacked coordination. Only 21 heavy bombers failed to return. This was just two more than the number claimed by the four Focke-Wulf *Gruppen* involved in the day's action (although a further 30 claims were submitted by other units!).

II./JG 26 was credited with three B-17s for one pilot wounded. I. and II./JG 1 managed to bring down a trio of Flying Fortresses between them – including a sixth for Feldwebel Heinz Fuchs – but it cost them four pilots killed and one wounded. By far the most successful of *any* Luftwaffe *Gruppe* engaged against the enemy on this 20 February was Hauptmann Rolf Hermichen's I./JG 11. At a price of just two pilots wounded, the unit's final tally for the day came to six B-17s and seven B-24s. Among the Flying Fortresses downed was a first for future *Viermot* ace Feldwebel Norbert Schuecking of 1. *Staffel* and a tenth for Feldwebel Alwin Doppler of 2. *Staffel*, while four of the seven Liberators were despatched by the *Gruppenkommandeur* alone in less than 20 minutes.

Twenty-four hours later it was the Luftwaffe's airfields in western Germany that were to have felt the weight of the enemy's bombs, but as

One of the two Flying Fortresses brought down by Heinz Bär on 22 February 1944 – the 91st BG's *'Miss Ouachita'* (OR-Q/42-3040), which crash-landed southeast of Osnabrück – is subjected to close scrutiny by the experts. Seen here inspecting the bomber's upper turret are, from left, Oberfeldwebel Leo Schuhmacher, now Bär's wingman (and sporting a captured US flying jacket), Major Bär himself, and Feldwebel Max Sauer, Oberst Oesau's regular wingman

had so often been the case in the past, operations were severely curtailed by that perennial foe of both sides – the weather. The Reich's Defence Fw 190s claimed a dozen of the 16 bomber losses admitted by the Eighth Air Force. II./JG 26's pair, one of them going to 'Addi' Glunz, were scored without loss. I./JG 11's three victories were all claimed by feldwebeln. Heinz Stöwer's Flying Fortress took his tally to five and made him an ace, while Alwin Doppler rang the changes by downing a Liberator to add to his long list of ten previous B-17s. Today's honours, however, went to JG 1. Its seven successes included a brace of Flying Fortresses for Major Heinz Bär, now officially installed as the *Kapitän* of 6. *Staffel.*

'Pritzl' Bär was credited with two more B-17s the following day, 22 February, as too was his *Geschwaderkommodore*, Oberst Walter 'Gulle' Oesau. This meant that JG 1's two most illustrious *Experten* had both become Fw 190 Defence of the Reich heavy bomber aces on the same date. Their achievement was overshadowed by that of Oberfeldwebel Adolf Glunz, the NCO *Staffelkapitän* of 5./JG 26, who submitted claims for a remarkable five(!) B-17s (including two *Herausschüsse*) and a single P-47 on this third day of 'Big Week'. Even though two of the bombers were subsequently disallowed, the remaining trio sufficed to bump Glunz's bomber tally up to ten.

Altogether, the Fw 190 *Gruppen* accounted for 27 of the 58 bombers claimed by the Luftwaffe on 22 February (which was 20 more than the enemy's actual losses). In addition to Bär's and Oesau's doubles, another four of JGs 1 and 11's total of 20 victories were credited to existing heavy bomber aces, the most successful of them being 3./JG 1's Leutnant Hans Ehlers, whose Flying Fortress, downed northwest of the Ruhr, took him to 13.

'Pritzl' Bär takes a moment to reflect on the damage done to the B-17's tail surfaces

The Eighth's primary objectives on 22 February had been aircraft factories in central Germany. The worsening weather put paid to a repeat performance the next day. While the Eighth stood down and the northern *Jagdgruppen* enjoyed a welcome breather, the heavy bombers of the Italian-based Fifteenth Air Force flew their second mission in support of the 'Big Week' offensive when they attacked the aircraft assembly and ball bearing plants at Steyr, in Austria, where their main opposition came from the Bf 109s of JGs 53 and 77.

On 24 February the Eighth returned to the fray with renewed raids on aviation industry and associated targets. It was to prove the most costly day of 'Big Week' for the Americans. Taking advantage of the clearing skies, the Luftwaffe was up in force, scrambling elements of 29 *Gruppen* in all. And it was the Liberators targeting the Bf 110 manufacturing facility at Gotha, in central Germany, that bore the brunt of their attacks, losing 33 of their number out of the 49 bombers that failed to return on this date.

The four Fw 190 *Gruppen* of JGs 1 and 11 claimed 20 Liberators between them. Major Emil-Rudolf Schnoor's I./JG 1, up from Twente in Holland, accounted for five. All went to established bomber aces – the *Gruppenkommandeur's* took his score to 12, while two oberfeldwebeln of 2. *Staffel*, Anton-Rudolf Piffer and Erich Demuth, raised their tallies to 18 and 9 respectively, and 1./JG 1's Unteroffizier Rudolf Hübl got a pair to take him to 13. These successes, however, had cost the *Gruppe* three pilots killed and two wounded.

Rheine-based II./JG 1 was credited with four B-24s, including

Another of the Eighth's Flying Fortresses that failed to return on 22 February 1944 – the third day of 'Big Week' – was the 381st BG's *'Friday the 13th'* (VE-M/42-31443), seen here in the foreground, lower left, during an earlier mission

Both 'Pritzl' Bär (left) and 'Gulle' Oesau (right) – pictured here together with Oberst Walter Grabmann, AOC 3. *Jagd-Division* – claimed their fifth Defence of the Reich heavy bombers on the same day, 22 February 1944

Oberfeldwebel Adolf 'Addi' Glunz, the caretaker NCO *Staffelkapitän* of 5./JG 26, chats to his mechanics. The imposing rudder scoreboard displays 54 aerial victories, the last of them presumably the Flying Fortress downed over the Dutch coast on 21 February 1944. Twenty-four hours later he would submit claims for no fewer than five B-17s and one P-47

Returning from the eastern front, where he had won the Oak Leaves as an oberfeldwebel for his 100+ victories, Josef 'Jupp' Zwernemann was to account for six Defence of the Reich heavy bombers during his nearly four months as *Staffelkapitän* of 1./JG 11

two for Heinz Bär. It also lost three pilots, one of them being Feldwebel Heinz Fuchs of 4./JG 1. A seven-victory bomber ace, Fuchs had been leading the *Staffel* on this mission and was last seen attacking a Liberator south of Minden.

While III./JG 11's sole success was a fourth Flying Fortress for 'Toni' Hackl, half of I./JG 11's ten Liberators were claimed by just two feldwebeln, both of 2. *Staffel* and both already bomber aces – Alwin Doppler's trio raised his score to 15 and Franz Steiner's pair took him to ten. Another B-24 went to the Oak Leaves-wearing *Staffelkapitän* of 1./JG 11. Although this was the *Kapitän's* first heavy bomber, it was his 119th victory of the war to date, for Oberleutnant Josef 'Jupp' Zwernemann was another of the high-scoring eastern front *Experten* of JG 52 who had been transferred back to the Reich to add his experience and expertise to the defence of the homeland.

The Fw 190 pilots of JG 26 submitted claims for nine heavy bombers, four of them Liberators. Two *Staffelkapitäne* added a B-24 each to their growing totals, which took 2./JG 26's Leutnant Karl 'Charly' Willius' total to five and 7./JG 26's Leutnant Waldemar 'Waldi' Radener's to eight. Oberleutnant Walter Matoni of 5. *Staffel* also claimed one of the B-24s. It was his fourth bomber. *Geschwader* records also indicated that the Liberator he had sent down 50 miles to the east of Bonn was JG 26's 2000th victory of the war.

In apparent recognition of this fact, Oberleutnant Matoni was rewarded by being made *Kapitän* of 5. *Staffel* the very next day.

And that day, 25 February, was to see the final mission of 'Big Week'. The primary targets for the enemy were the Messerschmitt plants in southern Germany. Although the Luftwaffe was up in larger numbers than ever before (claiming a staggering 112 heavy bombers against the Eighth and Fifteenth Air Forces' actual combined losses of 64), the Fw 190 units played only a minor role, with just two *Gruppen* reporting any successes. In addition to the two bombers credited to JG 1's *Geschwaderkommodore* Oberst Walter Oesau – a B-17 and a B-24 both downed near Baden-Baden – II./JG 1 claimed seven victories.

Major Heinz Bär was responsible for four of them. On his first sortie of the day he got a pair of Flying Fortresses, one an *Herausschuss* and the other a 'final destruction'. Later he added another B-17 *Herausschuss*, plus a B-24. The latter, which he shot down north of Karlsruhe, took 'Pritzl' Bär's heavy bomber score into double figures.

Meanwhile, II./JG 26 had claimed just five. A Liberator *Herausschuss* and the 'final destruction' of a Flying Fortress for the *Kapitän* of 7. *Staffel*, 'Waldi' Radener, raised his score to ten as well. As if to rub salt into the wound, the about-to-be-deposed *Staffelkapitän* of 5./JG 26, Oberfeldwebel 'Addi' Glunz, had his Flying Fortress disallowed.

So ended 'Big Week'. In its wake the skies of the Reich remained quiet as both sides paused to take stock. Bad weather prevented the Luftwaffe from going up against a small-scale raid on Brunswick on 29 February, which cost the attackers just one B-17 lost to flak. The Americans now had their sights set on the greatest propaganda target of all – Berlin.

After striking at Frankfurt on 2 March, when operations were again severely affected by the weather (among the handful of claims submitted by the defenders was a sixth heavy bomber for 2./JG 26's 'Charly' Willius), the Eighth set out 24 hours later on its first attempt to attack the German capital. The weather had not yet released its grip, however, and if anything it was getting worse. Solid high cloud prevented the bombers from penetrating very far inland. They were forced instead to seek targets of opportunity on or near the northern coast, including that favourite last resort of many, the already badly damaged Wilhelmshaven.

Of the 11 bombers that the Eighth admitted losing on 3 March, six were claimed by pilots of I./JG 11, which was one of the few *Gruppen* to make contact. Two of the unit's existing heavy bomber aces, *Gruppenkommandeur* Hauptmann Rolf Hermichen and 2. *Staffel*'s Feldwebel Alwin Doppler, each added a B-17 to his list. 'Jupp' Zwernemann of 1./JG 11, still a relative newcomer to Defence of the Reich operations, got his second bomber of the campaign.

The weather was still calling the shots the following day when the Eighth again tried to target Berlin. The B-24s had to abandon their part in the mission even before completing assembly, and most of the B-17s were forced to turn back after reaching the Ruhr. A small formation of some 30 Flying Fortresses did manage to make it to the greater Berlin area, scattering their bombs on the southwestern suburbs of the city. The damage they caused was slight, but it was to be a different story two days later when conditions finally relented and Eighth Air Force 'heavies' appeared over the capital of the Reich in force.

The clear blue skies that the Americans had been waiting for allowed the Germans to respond in kind. Not only did they put 25 *Gruppen* (plus

The B-24 that Oberleutnant Walter Matoni of 5./JG 26 claimed east of Bonn on 24 February 1944 was calculated to be JG 26's 2000th victory of the war to date. Apparently as a reward, Walter Matoni replaced Oberfeldwebel Adolf Glunz as the *Kapitän* of 5. *Staffel* the very next day. One can almost hear the conversation, Matoni (left), 'Sorry, "Addi", but the *Staffel's* all mine now'. Pure fantasy, of course – in fact, this shot was probably taken at the same time as the 'emergency scramble' pictured on page 57. 'Addi' Glunz had little cause for complaint, however, as he would be appointed *Staffelkapitän* of 6./JG 26 on 3 March and made up to leutnant shortly thereafter

several other smaller units) into the air, they were also able to form many of these into *Gefechtsverbände*, or massed 'battle formations'. The first such formation to engage the enemy was six-*Gruppen* strong, and it included the Focke-Wulfs of I. and II./JG 1 and I. and III./JG 11. Led by Hauptmann Rolf Hermichen of I./JG 11, this *Gefechtsverband* launched the first concerted frontal attack on the bombers over Haselünne shortly before noon, when the enemy were less than 20 miles inside Reich airspace. Scything through the serried ranks of B-17s, the German pilots claimed 16 Flying Fortresses in the space of just ten minutes. And in the next quarter-of-an-hour they downed 13 more.

The Americans admitted the loss of more than 20 bombers in these first furious engagements, with the luckless 100th BG – the 'Bloody Hundredth' – alone accounting for well over half that number. The list of claimants during the initial 25 minutes of the day's action reads like a roll call of Fw 190 Defence of the Reich heavy bomber aces present and future. The first success was almost certainly the B-17 credited to 'Jupp' Zwernemann at 1155 hrs. It was US bomber number three for the ex-eastern front *Experte*.

Formation leader Rolf Hermichen scored a trio (his Nos 13-15), while Hauptmann Hermann Segatz, the *Gruppenkommandeur* of II./JG 1 (5 and 6), 'Pritzl' Bär of 6./JG 1(11 and 12) and 2./JG 1's Oberfeldwebel Erich Demuth (10 and 11) claimed two each. Another five got a single Flying Fortress apiece, namely JG 1's *Geschwaderkommodore* Oberst Walter Oesau (9), Feldwebel Rudolf Hübl of 2./JG 1 (12), Feldwebel Walter Köhne of 3./JG 1 (9), Oberleutnant Hans-Heinrich Koenig, the *Staffelkapitän* of 3./JG 11 (11), and 7./JG 11's Oberfeldwebel Siegfried Zick (4).

Some 15 minutes after this opening round Leutnant Hans Ehlers, the *Staffelkapitän* of 3./JG 1, sent a Flying Fortress down north of Osnabrück to take his heavy bomber score to 14, but fellow-*Staffelkapitän* Oberleutnant Rüdiger Kirchmayr had to be content with a 'final destruction' to the southwest of Haselünne.

With the bomber stream disappearing eastwards as the 'heavies' continued to battle their way towards Berlin, it was time for the Focke-Wulf *Gruppen* to put down, refuel and re-arm in readiness to meet the enemy formations on their return flight. The Fw 190s re-established contact some two hours later as the Flying Fortresses passed to the south of Bremen heading back for the Dutch border. And once again it was 'Jupp' Zwernemann who claimed the first victim. 'Pritzl' Bär and 'King' Koenig also added another B-17 each to their day's scores.

Two NCO pilots of I./JG 11, Oberfeldwebel Heinz Stöwer of 3. *Staffel* and Feldwebel Alwin Doppler of 2. *Staffel*, were credited with a Flying Fortress each during this second phase of the battle (taking their respective heavy bomber scores to 7 and 17), while Oberfeldwebel Leo Schuhmacher – who was now Major Heinz Bär's regular wingman in 6./JG 1 – got his third. The most successful pilot of all was Oberleutnant Hugo Frey, the *Staffelkapitän* of 7./JG 11, who had claimed no fewer than four B-17s (possibly all from the 388th BG) over or near the German-Dutch border just before 1500 hrs. This raised Frey's tally of US heavy bombers to 26, the first 20 of which, however, had been scored on Bf 109s prior to III./JG 11's conversion to the Fw 190 in January.

As the retreating bombers approached the Dutch and Belgian borders they also came under attack from elements of JG 26. Three of the five claimants in the ensuing actions were *Staffelkapitäne*. 2./JG 26's Leutnant Karl Willius got a B-17 and Oberleutnant Wolfgang Neu of 4./JG 26 downed a B-24 (their seventh and fourth Defence of the Reich heavy bombers respectively). The last victim to fall to an Fw 190 was probably the unfortunate 381st BG Flying Fortress that had been damaged by both flak and fighter attack shortly before reaching the target area. For the past two hours it had been limping back across Germany, only to be caught and sent down west of Cologne by Oberleutnant Walter Matoni, the new *Staffelkapitän* of 5./JG 26. For some reason it was not recorded as a 'final destruction', but credited to Matoni as his fifth US bomber of the campaign.

The Luftwaffe claimed the destruction of 118 enemy bombers during this first American daylight raid on Berlin. Although the Eighth's true losses were just over half that figure, they still represented the highest single day's casualty rate ever to be suffered over Germany. In their turn, the Luftwaffe lost 66 aircraft, with 36 pilots killed and 27 wounded.

Among the six Fw 190 pilots known to have been killed in action were two *Viermot* aces. One was 4./JG 1's Oberfeldwebel Detlef Lüth, shot down east of Haselünne during the initial midday attack on the B-17s. The other was Oberleutnant Hugo Frey. Reportedly hit by return fire from the last of the four Flying Fortresses he had despatched, Frey himself went down to crash a few miles beyond the Dutch border. His loss was a hard blow, coming just four days after the death of JG 2's Oberstleutnant Egon Mayer, who had been shot down in a dogfight with P-47s over the French town of Montmédy. It meant that the Luftwaffe had suddenly lost its two leading anti-bomber *Experten*, most of whose victories, it should again perhaps be pointed out, had been achieved while flying the Bf 109.

The 6 March 1944 mission against Berlin has rightly been described as the real turning point in the Defence of the Reich campaign. Never again would the defenders be able to match the 69 American bombers destroyed on this date (although they would come close to doing so on two occasions in the month ahead). Heavy as the Eighth's losses had undoubtedly been, they could be borne. And not merely borne, but more than made good by the influx of new units, new aircraft and new personnel arriving from the US.

As the enemy's numbers grew – particularly the numbers of those all-important P-51 Mustang escort fighters – so the last 12 months of the Defence of the Reich took on a whole new resonance. Heavily escorted, the Eighth Air Force's bombers would soon be able, quite literally, to spread their wings into every corner of Hitler's Reich, striking at up to ten or more primary targets on a single day, and suffering ever fewer casualties as they did so.

Although the Luftwaffe tried hard to remain on terms with the growing might of the enemy – German fighter production would reach an all-time high in the autumn of 1944 – a battle of attrition against the industrial muscle and manpower of America was one battle it could not hope to win. The hard-pressed Focke-Wulf and Messerschmitt plants might still be turning out the fighters, but the pilots required to fly these

Another single-day multiple bomber ace was Oberleutnant Hugo Frey, the *Staffelkapitän* of 7./JG 11, who claimed four B-17s (verified by his wingman) during the Eighth Air Force's 6 March raid on Berlin before himself falling victim to the Flying Fortresses' return fire

machines in action were labouring under increasingly poor standards of training. This inadequacy was evidenced by the *Jagdgruppens'* lengthening casualty lists as their pilots attempted – and more often than not failed – to punch a way through the strong screen of enemy fighters to get at the bombers they were protecting.

As 1944 progressed, individual units' score sheets began to reflect this operational sea change. They began to include more and more fighter victories, interspersed by the occasional successful downing of a heavy bomber – a complete reversal of the situation that had existed throughout most of 1943.

Leaving aside the dedicated *Sturm* units, the Fw 190 pilots engaged against the Eighth Air Force's heavy bombers could now be broadly divided into three categories. Firstly, there was the *Nachwuchs* (the 'new growth', or newcomers), who would be used in increasing numbers to replace the growing losses suffered by the Defence of the Reich *Jagdgruppen*, particularly after the bloodletting of the Normandy campaign. Many of these youngsters, perfunctorily trained but full of fighting spirit, might be lucky enough to account for a couple of US heavy bombers – maybe three, or even four – before inevitably falling victim to the overwhelming might of the enemy.

Then there were those veterans of the 15-month-old campaign who had claimed their first bomber successes over the North Sea back at the beginning of 1943 and had since seen their scores grow into double figures. Their undeniable experience was no longer a guarantee of continued survival, however, and many familiar names would feature on the loss returns in the months ahead. Finally, there was that handful

On 8 March, during the Eighth Air Force's second visit to Berlin, Hauptmann Rolf Hermichen, the *Gruppenkommandeur* of I./JG 11, emulated Hugo Frey's performance when he too downed four bombers – two B-17s and two B-24s. Unlike Frey, however, he lived to tell the tale, and is seen here being carried in triumph by jubilant members of his groundcrew after landing back at Rotenburg

of truly stellar individuals, highly decorated pilots with scores of 100 or more, who were transferred in from other theatres – predominantly the Russian front – to take over positions of command within the Defence of the Reich organisation. Some of these proven *Experten* adapted to their new environment better than others, but not even they were immune to the ferocity of the air war now being waged in the skies above Germany.

Lack of space precludes further day-by-day itemisation of the many savage and complex battles still to be fought in the Defence of the Reich campaign. Attention must now perforce be focused on the individual aces of that campaign; not only those who already had five or more heavy bombers to their credit, but also those – far fewer in number – who had yet to achieve that status.

Two days after the 6 March raid on Berlin the Eighth returned to 'Big B', as the American crews had quickly dubbed the German capital. This time the attackers lost 37 of their bombers, with the Luftwaffe's Fw 190 aces accounting for ten of them (plus eight fighters). I./JG 11's Rolf Hermichen outdid his performance of 48 hours earlier by bringing down four heavy bombers, two B-17s and two B-24s. One of Hermichen's

Staffelkapitäne, Oberleutnant Josef Zwernemann of 1./JG 11, claimed two victories. One was a P-47 but the other, a B-17, provided 'Jupp' Zwernemann with his fifth heavy bomber. Another *Staffelkapitän*, 5./JG 26's Oberleutnant Walter Matoni, got a brace of Flying Fortresses. The three pilots credited with a single bomber each were Hauptmann Hermann Segatz, the *Gruppenkommandeur* of II./JG 1, Oberleutnant Rüdiger Kirchmayr, the *Staffelkapitän* of 5./JG 1, and future *Experte* Feldwebel Norbert Schuecking of 1./JG 11 (the latter claiming his second B-17).

Segatz and Kirchmayr had both accounted for B-24s, although the former's victim was, in fact, an *Herausschuss*, which he shot out of a Liberator formation to the south of Berlin. It was to be Hermann Segatz's seventh and last heavy bomber victory, for his own 'White 23' was hit by return fire during the encounter and crashed near Luckau.

Experienced unit leaders like Segatz were becoming increasingly difficult to replace. And it was this harsh fact, rather than any change of heart on the part of the Luftwaffe's powers-that-be, that persuaded them to overlook Major Heinz Bär's supposed previous 'misdemeanours' and appoint him *Gruppenkommandeur* of II./JG 1 in place of the fallen Segatz just over a week later. The ebullient 'Pritzl' Bär's career was on the way up again!

Hermann Segatz was the fourth and last Fw 190 heavy bomber ace to be lost in March 1944. The Eighth was to fly ten more missions over the Reich – suffering bomber losses ranging from 43 to just one – before the month was out. Conditions permitting, the Luftwaffe's *Jagdgruppen* continued to offer determined resistance, with a number of Focke-Wulf pilots reaching further milestones in their anti-bomber careers.

On 18 March – the day the Americans lost 43 bombers (28 of them Liberators) attacking aviation industry targets in southern Germany – 3./JG 26's Oberfeldwebel Erich Scheyda claimed his sixth, and final, bomber victory when he downed a 100th BG Flying Fortress near Ulm. Scheyda would be killed in action against RCAF Spitfires over France on 7 May. Another B-17 downed southwest of Ulm on 18 March was the tenth – and also the last – *Viermot* success for Hauptmann Herbert Huppertz, the newly appointed *Gruppenkommandeur* of III./JG 2.

Hauptmann Herbert Huppertz (left), *Gruppenkommandeur* of III./JG 2, gained his tenth and last Defence of the Reich heavy bomber victory southwest of Ulm on 18 March 1944

Meanwhile, south of Freiburg, the Focke-Wulfs of I. and III./JG 11 had intercepted an unescorted formation of B-24s returning from a raid on Friedrichshafen, on the shores of Lake Constance. The Fw 190s launched a coordinated, classic '12 o'clock-high' frontal attack on the US bombers. By the time they broke off the engagement they had accounted for 19 of the B-24s. Several of the two units' existing aces added to their lengthening lists of kills, while the first of the trio of Liberators credited to Hauptmann Anton Hackl – his 137th victory of the war to date – gave the *Kommandeur* of III./JG 11 his fifth heavy bomber since the *Gruppe's* conversion to Fw 190s.

Five days later, on 23 March, two more of JG 11's future *Experten* took their bomber tallies to five when

The trio of Liberators credited to III./JG 11's *Gruppenkommandeur* Hauptmann Anton Hackl on 18 March 1944 took his overall score to 139 and the number of heavy bombers he had brought down since his *Gruppe's* recent conversion to Fw 190s to seven. 'Toni' Hackl is seen here (left) some five months earlier in the company of Major Anton Mader, JG 11's first *Geschwaderkommodore*

1. *Staffel's* Feldwebel Norbert Schuecking claimed a pair of B-17s (Nos 5 and 6) and Oberfeldwebel Siegfried Zick of 7. *Staffel* got a Liberator. All four Fw 190 *Gruppen* of JGs 1 and 11 were in action on this date, which saw the Eighth Air Force attacking a range of targets in northwest Germany, and their aces accounted for ten of the 17 bombers claimed. 3./JG 1's Feldwebel Walter Köhne was credited with his tenth when he downed a B-17 near Osnabrück. Finally, both Hauptmann Rolf Hermichen, the *Gruppenkommandeur* of I./JG 11, and Feldwebel Alwin Doppler of 2. *Staffel* attained two kills apiece, thus taking their bomber scores to 20.

Hermichen's victim – a Flying Fortress sent down south of Bremen – was his 61st victory overall. Alwin Doppler's performance was perhaps all the more remarkable in that the B-17 he despatched west of Celle provided only the 20th entry on his score sheet, with *all* 19 of his previous successes also being US four-engined bombers!

The month ended with a raid by 200+ Flying Fortresses on Brunswick. Among the 16 victories claimed by the Focke-Wulfs of JGs 1 and 11 – ten bombers and six fighters – was a fifth heavy bomber for 1./JG 11's Oberfähnrich Gerhard Dreizehner. His was another promising career that was soon to be cut short, for he was shot down over Schleswig-Holstein during the Americans' 9 April raid on aviation plants along the Baltic coast.

The Eighth kept up the pressure during April with 13 missions against the Reich. The strength of the Luftwaffe's response may be gauged from the fact that this was the month in which, for the last time in the campaign, its pilots were able to claim more than 60 enemy bombers in a single day. Indeed, it was to happen twice. They downed 64 bombers during the Eighth Air Force's strikes on Focke-Wulf and Junkers aircraft factories on 11 April, before accounting for another 63 during the Berlin raid of 29 April.

All this activity gave the Fw 190 aces plenty of opportunities to increase their scores, which many of them did. The month's successes were to come at a high price, however. 8 April saw the Eighth's Flying Fortresses attacking a number of Luftwaffe airfields in northwest Germany, while the Liberators concentrated on aircraft manufacturing and assembly plants around Brunswick. Despite the support of almost 800 fighters, more than a quarter of them P-51s, the Americans lost 34 bombers on this date. All but four of them came from the ranks of the luckless Liberators targeting Brunswick.

Of the nearly two dozen B-24s claimed by the Focke-Wulfs of JGs 1 and 11 in a savage, 20-minute battle near Salzwedel, one gave 2./JG 1's Oberfeldwebel Anton-Rudolf Piffer his 20th bomber kill of the campaign. A second fell to Oberleutnant Georg-Peter Eder. Another somewhat controversial figure, 'Schorsch' Eder had been appointed *Staffelkapitän* of 6./JG 1 upon Heinz Bär's elevation to the command of II./JG 1. Recently recovered from severe injuries, Eder had previously served with both JG 51 in Russia and JG 2 on the Channel coast. And although he already had 11 heavy bombers under his belt, the B-24 he sent down southwest of Salzwedel was the first the ace had scored while flying Fw 190s in Defence of the Reich.

JG 1's 14 Liberators had cost it just two pilots killed, but JG 11 did not escape so lightly. Its eight bombers had resulted in 11 pilots dead and two wounded, for after carrying out an initial head-on attack on the B-24s, the two *Gruppen's* Focke-Wulfs had been pounced upon by a large force of Mustang escorts. Oberleutnant Josef Zwernemann, *Staffelkapitän* of 1./JG 11, managed to down both a Liberator (his sixth heavy bomber) and one of the aggressive P-51s all in the space of little more than 60 seconds, but then his own 'White 11' fell victim to another pair of Mustangs. The 126-victory 'Jupp' Zwernemann was seen to bail out over Gardelegen, only to be shot in his parachute by one of the American fighters.

Almost exactly one-and-a-half hours after Zwernemann's Liberator had been despatched west of Salzwedel, the formation of B-24s – still heavily escorted and now just about to re-cross the Dutch border on their return flight – suffered another frontal attack, this time by the Fw 190s of I./JG 26. The assault was led by Leutnant Karl Willius, the *Kapitän* of 2. *Staffel*, who was the only pilot able to claim one of the bombers. It proved to be 'Charly' Willius' tenth and final Defence of the Reich *Viermot* success, for like Zwernemann before him, he too was almost immediately set upon by US fighters. Willius' wingman, under attack himself, lost sight of his leader after observing him dive away with a Thunderbolt glued to his tail. It would be 23 years before Leutnant Karl Willius' remains were found in the wreckage of his 'Black 5', buried deep in the soft Dutch polder less than two miles from the German border.

Despite losses such as these, and others yet to come, April and May 1944 were undoubtedly the most successful two months of the entire campaign for the Focke-Wulf aces. During that time eight new pilots joined their ranks by each claiming a fifth heavy bomber, and eight more took their scores into double figures. Another half-dozen got their 15th, one his 20th, and the leading pair both achieved their quarter-century.

On 8 April, the day Willius and Zwernemann were lost, 3./JG 1's Oberleutnant Hans Ehlers and Oberfeldwebel Leo Schuhmacher of 6./JG 1 – both future Knight's Cross winners – downed a B-24 each during the Salzwedel encounter to become heavy bomber aces. Twenty-four hours later, when the Eighth struck at aviation plants in eastern Germany and Poland, the now Major Rudolf-Emil Schnoor, *Gruppenkommandeur* of I./JG 1, claimed a B-24 over the Fehmarn Belt between Germany and Denmark as the bombers headed east into the Baltic towards their targets. It was the 15th *Viermot* of his career. Just over four hours later, three of the B-17s making for home through the same area provided tenth victories for Hauptmann Alfred Grislawski of 8./JG 1 and for Oberleutnant Hans-Heinrich Koenig and Feldwebel Heinz Stöwer, both of 3./JG 11.

During the Eighth's costly mission against the Focke-Wulf and Junkers aircraft factories on 11 April, the Fw 190 aces claimed at least a dozen of

Like Herbert Huppertz seen on page 68, Leutnant Karl Willius, the *Staffelkapitän* of 2./JG 26, would achieve exactly ten Defence of the Reich heavy bomber victories before being killed in action against P-47 Thunderbolts. The loss of the popular 'Charly' Willius on 8 April 1944 was keenly felt by all. Below the cockpit sill of the Fw 190 shown here are the flags of the countries he had fought against at the start of his career when with JG 51, namely Holland, Belgium and France

the 64 enemy bombers that were lost. Major Schnoor was credited with

a brace of Flying Fortresses, while one of his *Staffelkapitäne*, Oberleutnant Rudolf Engleder of 2./JG 1, downed a Liberator. This was to be Engleder's 17th and final heavy bomber of the Defence of the Reich campaign. Four days later he was posted away to assume command of a fighter-training unit in France. He was one of the very few anti-bomber *Experten* to be taken off operational flying, and thus be able to impart his knowledge and experience to the next generation of young trainees.

After the heavy casualties of 11 April, the Eighth's bomber crews were given a brief respite when another deep-penetration raid planned for the following day had to be abandoned due to the weather. The B-17 formations were recalled just as they were crossing the French coast, but the B-24s had got as far as the German border before being ordered to turn back for home. Five of them did not make it. Two fell victim to French-based *Staffelkapitäne*, namely 9./JG 2's Oberleutnant Josef Wurmheller and 8./JG 26's Leutnant Wilhelm Hofmann, thereby raising both to ace status.

The next day, 13 April, the Eighth made it to Schweinfurt and other targets in southern Germany, losing 38 heavy bombers in the process. Feldwebel Gerhard Vogt of 7./JG 26 also joined the ranks of the aces on this date by being credited with a Flying Fortress *Herausschuss* near Trier. Two minutes later and some 20 miles away to the west of Bitburg, a similar

claim gave a tenth bomber kill to Oberleutnant Walter Matoni, the *Staffelkapitän* of 5./JG 26.

13 April was also to see the last Defence of the Reich heavy bomber successes for both Oberstleutnant Josef Priller, *Geschwaderkommodore* of JG 26, and Major Emil-Rudolf Schnoor, *Gruppenkommandeur* of I./JG 1. The Flying Fortresses were the two COs' third and 18th such *Viermots* respectively.

While the redoubtable 'Pips' Priller remained at the head of his *Geschwader* until being given a staff

The fifth Defence of the Reich heavy bomber for Oberleutnant Josef 'Sepp' Wurmheller was a B-24 claimed on 12 April 1944

The normally effervescent 'Pips' Priller, *Geschwaderkommodore* of JG 26, rarely seemed to smile when being photographed, so the news contained in the message he is reading here must have been particularly good to prompt such a happy grin. Note, incidentally, the cloth pilot's badge sewn on the pocket of his leather flying jacket

Oberstleutnant Josef Priller and Major Emil-Rudolf Schnoor, *Gruppenkommandeur* of I./JG 1, both claimed their last Defence of the Reich heavy bomber victories on 13 April 1944. 'Pips' Priller would go on to achieve further successes, but Major Schnoor's operational career came to an abrupt end three days later when he clipped a tree during a low-level training session. This is the wreckage of his 'White 20' in which he was seriously injured while attempting to make an emergency landing near Detmold

'BIG WEEK', BERLIN AND OIL

appointment late in January 1945, Major Schnoor's operational career was brought to an abrupt end on 16 April when he suffered severe injuries during a training flight.

Eight days after Schnoor's accident, two B-17s lost during the Eighth Air Force's maximum-effort mission aimed at airfields and associated targets in southern Germany took Georg-Peter Eder's rapidly rising score to five.

On 29 April the American bombers returned to Berlin. Nearly a quarter of the 63 machines they lost were claimed by the Fw 190 aces of JGs 1 and 11. Leutnant Hans Schrangl of I./JG 1 was welcomed into their ranks on this date with a B-24 *Herausschuss* southeast of Bremen, while a B-17 downed east of Brunswick took the score of 2./JG 1's Oberfeldwebel Rudolf Hübl to 15. 29 April was noteworthy too for being the day on which Oberleutnant Hans-Heinrich Koenig, the *Staffelkapitän* of 3./JG 11, famously claimed four heavy bombers – all B-24s, and all in the Nienburg-Hannover area – which raised his total to 16. It also marked the end of a chapter in two more Defence of the Reich careers.

The B-17 *Herausschuss* credited to 7./JG 26's *Staffelkapitän* Oberleutnant Waldemar Radener was his 13th heavy bomber of the campaign. He would be severely wounded in action against a formation of Liberators attacking a target in France on 11 May. Returning to the command of his *Staffel* in September, 'Waldi' Radener would claim just

A 452nd BG Flying Fortress over Berlin's Tempelhof airport during the 29 April 1944 raid on the German capital

two more heavy bombers – RAF Lancasters engaged in a daylight raid on Cologne on 23 December – before his transfer to JG 300 early in 1945.

And the B-24 that Major Heinz Bär, the *Gruppenkommandeur* of II./JG 1, got east of Brunswick on the morning of 29 April was not only his 202nd victory of the war to date, but also his 17th and final Fw 190 Defence of the Reich bomber success. On 1 June he would be appointed *Geschwaderkommodore* of JG 3 (with whom he downed three Allied fighters) before – in typical Bär fashion – he went back down to *Gruppenkommandeur* to take command of III./EJG 2, an Me 262 jet fighter training unit, in February 1945. He added two last Liberators to his overall score while flying the twinjet Me 262.

By a strange quirk of fate, both 'Waldi' Radener and 'Pritzl' Bär were to lose their lives in flying accidents – Radener in a T-6 Texan trainer of the new Bundesluftwaffe and Bär while demonstrating a light sports aircraft at Brunswick, scene of his final Fw 190 *Viermot* success – within four months of each other early in 1957.

4 May 1944 saw the award of the first Knight's Cross directly relating to a Defence of the Reich Fw 190 pilot. Sadly, the decoration was posthumous, being conferred upon Hugo Frey of JG 11, who had been killed in action nearly two months previously.

The Eighth Air Force's twin strikes against Berlin and Brunswick on 8 May were again vigorously contested by JGs 1 and 11. The two units' Focke-Wulf aces were credited with 11 of the enemy's 36 admitted bomber losses. The first of the two B-17s that Major Anton Hackl brought down southeast of Bremen took the *Gruppenkommandeur* of III./JG 11's Fw 190 heavy bomber score into double figures. Oberst Walter Oesau, the *Geschwaderkommodore* of JG 1, claimed one of the bombers' escorting P-47s in the same area. It was to be the last of his 118 wartime victories.

Three days later the whole of JG 1 was scrambled to engage US bombers attacking railway targets in northeastern France. The unit failed to achieve a single success, while losing at least seven of its own fighters, among them 'Green 13', the *Kommodore's* Bf 109G-6. After his wingman's aircraft had been damaged and was forced to break away, 'Gulle' Oesau fought a lone, 20-minute battle with a gaggle of P-38 Lightnings before finally succumbing close to the Belgian-German border. His death came as a massive blow to the *Geschwader*, which was subsequently named JG 1 'Oesau' in his honour.

Ever since 'Big Week' back in February, the Eighth Air Force had been striving to weaken Germany's air defences by returning time and again to her aircraft factories and to the Luftwaffe's airfields. On 12 May the Americans suddenly turned their attention to a strategic objective of a different kind – the Reich's oil industry. The regular strikes against Axis oil targets would be an ever-recurring theme in the daylight bombing offensive from now until the closing weeks of the war. Records indicate that no fewer than 150 such missions would be mounted – 88 by the Eighth Air Force and 62 by the Fifteenth Air Force flying up from Italy – between 12 May 1944 and 20 April 1945. And the results, unlike those achieved against the aviation industry, would prove devastating. Germany continued to produce aircraft, but at war's end they would be found standing idle in their hundreds, grounded by a lack of fuel.

29 April 1944 brought the last *Viermot* success for 'Pritzl' Bär in the Fw 190. On 20 May he would relinquish his temporary command of JG 1 (which he had led for nine days as acting-*Kommodore* following the loss of Oberst Walter Oesau) and take over as *Geschwaderkommodore* of JG 3

Hugo Frey was honoured with a posthumous Knight's Cross on 4 May 1944 for his long and successful career in Defence of the Reich. Six of his 26 heavy bomber victories had been gained while flying the Fw 190

The loss of Oberst Walter Oesau on 11 May 1944 marked the end of an illustrious chapter in the history of *Jagdgeschwader* 1. Here, a youthful 'Gulle' Oesau is caught in pensive mood as he surveys the wreckage of one of the kills he claimed early in his career – almost certainly the No 615 Sqn Hurricane II that he shot down near Desvres on 5 February 1941 when *Gruppenkommandeur* of III./JG 3

Newly-fledged anti-bomber ace Oberfeldwebel Erwin Laskowski (far left) of 8./JG 11 – whose fifth kill was a Flying Fortress downed during the Eighth Air Force's 22 May 1944 raid on Kiel – listens intently as another of the *Staffel's* pilots recalls the mission just flown

Flown on 12 May, the opening round of the 'Oil Blitz' was an Eighth affair targeting six refineries in the Leipzig area of eastern central Germany. The Luftwaffe rose in force to defend these crucially important installations. Between them, the 18 *Gruppen* involved claimed a wildly optimistic 108 bomber successes (the Americans' true losses were 46). Once again, the four Fw 190 *Gruppen* of JGs 1 and 11 played an integral part in the action. A number of the units' aces added to their scores, including 3./JG 1's Oberfähnrich Walter Köhne, whose B-24 took his tally to 15. Leutnant Hans-Georg Güthenke of 3./JG 11 was credited with his fifth when he destroyed a B-17 in a head-on attack east of Koblenz, but the uncontrollable Flying Fortress, its left wing shot off, reared up directly into Güthenke's path before he had time to break away. He collided with the bomber's almost vertical right wing and, although he managed to bail out, the ace suffered serious injuries.

Oberfeldwebel Heinz Stöwer, one of 3./JG 11's veteran NCO pilots, got his 15th a week later when he claimed a B-17 *Herausschuss* north of Kiel on 19 May. And during the Eighth's next mission – another major raid on Kiel flown three days after that – a new ace emerged with Oberfeldwebel Erwin Laskowski of 8./JG 11 claiming his fifth *Viermot* success with the destruction of a B-17. Forty-eight hours later still, during the course of the Eighth Air Force's 24 May mission to Berlin, two Flying Fortresses upped the scores of 5./JG 1's Oberleutnant Rüdiger Kirchmayr and 3./JG 11's Leutnant Hans Schrangl to ten apiece. Still in the lead was the seemingly unstoppable Oberfeldwebel Alwin Doppler of 2./JG 11, whose B-17 on this date took his tally to 25.

For I./JG 11 the day's successes were completely overshadowed by the loss of the unit's newly-appointed *Gruppenkommandeur*, the popular Oberleutnant Hans-Heinrich 'King' Koenig. The weather conditions to the southwest of Kiel were described as abysmal – 'soup' in the Luftwaffe vernacular – as Koenig led his unit in arrowhead formation in a frontal attack against one of the boxes of Flying Fortresses heading for Berlin. The one-eyed Koenig must have misjudged his distance in the treacherous visibility, for suddenly there was the bright flash of an explosion as he collided

head-on with his intended victim. His Focke-Wulf, minus one wing, was last glimpsed fluttering down into the solid cloud below.

Five days later, on 29 May, the Eighth sent nearly 1000 bombers to eight aviation and oil targets in eastern Germany. Sixteen *Gruppen* of Luftwaffe fighters, including the Fw 190s of JG s 1 and 11, rose to meet them. The defenders claimed 55 bombers – 21 more than were actually lost – with the Focke-Wulfs accounting for 19 of them.

Three existing Fw 190 aces were credited with the last heavy bombers of their Defence of the Reich careers on this date. In a running battle fought along the Baltic coast against a formation of B-24s heading for the synthetic oil plant at Pölitz, 7./JG 11's Oberfeldwebel Siegfried Zick got a pair of Liberators, the first an *Herausschuss*, in the space of seven minutes. These took his final bomber score of the campaign to nine. Siegfried Zick would add at least four more Soviet aircraft to his tally during III./JG 11's forthcoming service on the eastern front, before being shot down with serious wounds on 18 July 1944.

Forty minutes after Zick's double success and 200 miles away to the south, Oberleutnant Georg-Peter Eder, now the *Gruppenkommandeur* of II./JG 1, downed a B-17 near Görlitz to bring his Defence of the Reich heavy bomber score on Fw 190s up into double figures. Having previously accounted for 11 Flying Fortresses while flying Bf 109s with JG 2 during 1942/43, Eder would go on to submit claims for another 14 B-17s (plus four probables) as an Me 262 jet pilot in the closing months of the war. If correct, these would put him on a par with (or, depending on the probables, even ahead of) the Luftwaffe's foremost heavy bomber claimant, Oberst Walther Dahl of *Sturm* fame.

The third pilot to bring his heavy bomber account to a close on this 29 May was Anton-Rudolf Piffer, the long-serving NCO of 2./JG 1, who had been promoted to leutnant and appointed *Kapitän* of 1. *Staffel* on 1 May. The Flying Fortress that Piffer shot down south of Berlin raised his *Viermot* tally to 26 (he had reached his quarter-century 24 hours earlier when credited with a B-17 near Magdeburg). All his bomber victories had been achieved on Defence of the Reich operations. His first, admittedly somewhat suspect, claim had been the Flying Fortress that he misidentified as a Short Stirling back in May 1943.

After having opened his score sheet with an RAF machine – the Mosquito of No 105 Sqn that he had sent down northwest of Osnabrück on 19 September 1942 – 'Toni' Piffer would end it in similar fashion, claiming a brace of Spitfires over Normandy on 16 June. He would himself then fall victim to Mustangs in a dogfight near Argentan the following day.

30 May witnessed the Eighth Air Force's last incursion into Reich airspace prior to D-Day. Among the targets attacked were a number of aircraft plants and Luftwaffe airfields in northwest Germany, including I./JG 11's base at

Fate finally caught up with the one-eyed Hans-Heinrich 'King' Koenig when he collided with a Flying Fortress in poor visibility southwest of Kiel on 22 May 1944. He too would be honoured with a posthumous Knight's Cross

The 95th BG's *'Ol' Dog'* (BG-Q/42-31924) was one of 34 heavy bombers that failed to return on 29 May 1944. Although the four Fw 190 *Gruppen* of JGs 1 and 11 claimed 14 Flying Fortresses (and five Liberators) on this date, the shrapnel damage to *'Ol' Dog's'* tail would seem to suggest that flak played at least a part in its demise

Rotenburg, near Bremen. The Focke-Wulfs of JGs 1 and 11 were again among the 13 *Jagdgruppen* scrambled in response, but their performance gives a graphic indication of the state to which they were now reduced. Neither I./JG 1 nor I./JG 11 managed to score any victories. II./JG 1 claimed a single P-51, while III./JG 11 were credited with a pair of B-24s. One of the latter provided 8. *Staffel's* Oberfeldwebel Erwin Laskowski with his seventh, and final, heavy bomber of the campaign, although he too would go on to achieve four more kills against the Red Air Force.

In return for these rather meagre successes, the four Focke-Wulf *Gruppen* suffered a total of five pilots killed and one wounded. They also lost at least 24 aircraft, the majority of them destroyed on the ground by bombing and strafing. One of those killed was 3./JG 11's Fahnenjunker-Oberfeldwebel Heinz Stöwer, who perished in a low-level dogfight with a pack of Mustangs to the north of Magdeburg. With 15 heavy bombers to his credit, the death of Stöwer – a long-serving NCO and experienced formation leader, now in line for a commission – effectively wrote *finis* to this main phase of the Fw 190s' hard-fought campaign against the Eighth's Flying Fortresses and Liberators.

Exactly one week after his loss, Allied troops stormed ashore on the beaches of Normandy and, in accordance with long-laid Luftwaffe plans, nearly all of the Defence of

Seen here (left) near the start of his career – note the early 'Devil in the clouds' badge of I./JG 1 (the ex-IV./JG 1) on the wall behind him – Anton-Rudolf Piffer subsequently rose to become the highest scoring of all Fw 190 Defence of the Reich anti-bomber *Experten*. Belated recognition of this achievement would come in the form of a posthumous Knight's Cross on 20 October 1944. The figure on the far right in the light flying jacket is Oberleutnant Hans Munz, *Staffelkapitän* of 1./JG 1, who was killed in action against B-17s during the Eighth Air Force's 21 May 1943 raid on Wilhelmshaven

Back to even earlier days with this shot of the then Unteroffizier Heinz Stöwer of 9./JG 1 celebrating his very first victory – a Coastal Command Beaufort brought down off Norway on 17 May 1942. After 9./JG 1's redesignation as 3./JG 11 on 1 April 1943, he would add 15 more kills to his tally (*all* US heavy bombers) before being caught by P-51s on 30 May 1944

the Reich *Jagdgruppen* were rushed westwards into France to help the Wehrmacht push them back. Three of JGs 1 and 11's four Fw 190 *Gruppen* were part of this mass redeployment (with III./JG 11 being despatched eastwards to perform the similarly hopeless task of trying to halt the Soviet advance).

After months of battling against US heavy bombers at high altitude, the Focke-Wulfs now abruptly found themselves having to face low-level Allied fighters and fighter-bombers. Despite this, and although vastly outnumbered, the three *Gruppen* put up a brave performance, claiming more than 70 enemy aircraft before June was out. But the price they paid was extortionate, with more than 30 pilots killed or missing, plus many others captured or seriously wounded.

Two victims of the Normandy air war, Hauptmann Herbert Huppertz, *Gruppenkommandeur* of III./JG 2, brought down by P-47s near Caen on D+2 . . .

One of the early casualties was Hauptmann Siegfried Simsch, who had been brought in to replace the fallen 'King' Koenig as the *Gruppenkommandeur* of I./JG 11 on 1 June. He lasted exactly a week before being shot down by P-51s east of Rennes on D+2. Nor was it solely the new arrivals in France who were falling victim to the Allies' overwhelming air superiority. On that same 8 June Channel front veteran Hauptmann Herbert Huppertz, *Gruppenkommandeur* of III./JG 2, was killed in action against P-47s near Caen. His successor at the head of III./JG 2 was Hauptmann Josef 'Sepp' Wurmheller. He too was to lose his life in the Caen area after colliding with his wingman during a dogfight to the south of the city on 22 June.

. . . and his successor at the head of III./JG 2, Hauptmann Josef 'Sepp' Wurmheller, who was lost in a mid-air collision during a dogfight exactly two weeks later

While the air battle for Normandy was raging, a clutch of awards had been announced. Although none related specifically to recent Defence of the Reich operations, four of the recipients were, in fact, Fw 190 aces of that campaign. Two of the decorations were posthumous – 'Charly' Willius' Knight's Cross on 9 June and Herbert Huppertz's Oak Leaves on 24 June. The latter date also saw Oak Leaves going to JG 26's 'Addi' Glunz, as well as a Knight's Cross for 'Schorsch' Eder, the *Gruppenkommandeur* of II./JG 1.

By this time the bombers of the Eighth Air Force , which for much of the past three weeks had been lending their not inconsiderable weight almost exclusively to the support of the Normandy invasion forces, were beginning to reappear in the skies over Germany. Their target on 24 June was Bremen. Of the 250+ Flying Fortresses that attacked the city's oil installations only one was brought down. It was a sad reflection of things that once had been, and a grim foretaste of things that were still to come.

THE LONG ROAD TO DEFEAT

During the high and late summer of 1944, while the bulk of the *Jagdgruppen* that had hitherto been the backbone of the Defence of the Reich organisation were being bled white in Normandy, the only Focke-Wulfs defending the homeland were the heavily armed and armoured machines of the *Sturmgruppen* (for more details see *Osprey Aviation Elite Units 20 - Luftwaffe Sturmgruppen*).

It was not until German forces were driven out of Normandy in the latter half of August that the survivors of the defending *Jagdgruppen* began to withdraw from France, some via the Low Countries, back into the Reich. For the majority of them there now perforce followed lengthy periods of re-equipment and retraining as they were returned to strength – at least numerically – by large intakes of undeniably keen but chronically undertrained new young pilots.

It was during this period that the individual *Gruppen* of JGs 1 and 11 were each increased to a four-*Staffel* complement to bring them into line with JGs 2 and 26, those long-term residents of France who, by the beginning of September 1944, had also been transferred back to airfields in Germany. Although they were all now stationed within the Reich's borders, there continued to be a distinction between the 'western' *Gruppen*, controlled by II. *Jagdkorps* still for the moment ensconced in its HQ at Rochefort, in Belgium, and the 'traditional' Defence of the Reich units commanded by I. *Jagddivision* at Döberitz.

Like the earlier edict concerning the division of labour between Bf 109 and Fw 190 units during anti-bomber missions, this bureaucratic delineation worked better on paper than it did in practice. In reality, *all* non-*Sturm* Focke-Wulf *Gruppen* based in western and central Germany would spend the final months of the war engaged primarily against the fighters and medium bombers of the Allies' tactical air forces. Apart from the occasional encounter, the Fw 190's campaign against the *Viermots* was, to all intents and purposes, over.

One of the first of those 'occasional encounters' was to take place during the latest of the Eighth Air Force's ongoing attacks on the Reich's oil industry. Among the targets on 12 September were the hydrogenation plants at Böhlen, Brüx and Ruhland. The Americans lost 35 of the nearly 900 bombers despatched, some two-dozen of that number being downed by fighters. The Luftwaffe had put 14 *Jagdgruppen* into the air to oppose the enemy. Of the six units flying Fw 190s, three were *Sturmgruppen*. The others were I./JG 2, I./JG 11 and II./JG 6 (the latter an *ex-Zerstörergruppe* recently converted to single-seaters).

I./JG 2 and I./JG 11 formed part of a *Gefechtsverband*. But neither *Gruppe* got anywhere near the bombers. While still assembling over the Wiesbaden area they were attacked by a large force of roving Mustangs.

In the aftermath of Normandy Hauptmann Walter Matoni relinquished command of I./JG 11 to become *Gruppenkommandeur*, first of I./JG 2 and then II./JG 2, until a serious crash in February 1945 rendered him unfit for further operational flying

The officer who took over from Walter Matoni at I./JG 11 was Hauptmann Bruno Stolle, a Channel front veteran who had four years' service with JG 2 behind him. This shot of Stolle at the salute must have been taken some time between 17 March 1943, the day he received his Knight's Cross, and 20 July 1944 . . .

In the fierce dogfights that ensued Major Erich Hohagen's I./JG 2 was able to claim a single P-51 for the loss of eight pilots. I./JG 11, now commanded by Hauptmann Walter Matoni, performed slightly better. It was credited with six Mustangs destroyed for the loss of two pilots killed and two wounded, but seven of the *Gruppe's* fighters were lost or written off.

There was, however, one Defence of the Reich ace who was successful on 12 September, but the pair of Flying Fortresses that Hauptmann Alfred Grislawski shot down north of Berlin did not add to his Focke-Wulf score sheet. He had been posted away from JG 1 exactly one month earlier and was now serving as the *Staffelkapitän* of the Bf 109-equipped 11./JG 53.

Nine days after this, on 21 September, a trio of familiar names from the ranks of JG 26 also increased their post-Normandy scores. These victories did not contribute to their final *Viermot* totals either, for the enemy aircraft credited to 'Addi' Glunz, Wilhelm Hofmann and Gerhard Vogt on this date were not four-engined bombers. They were three of the 20(!) unarmed RAF Dakota transports attempting to drop reinforcements to the British 1st Airborne Division surrounded at Arnhem that were hacked down by pilots of I. and II./JG 26 in ten minutes of pure slaughter.

The I./JG 2 and I./JG 11 *Gefechtsverband* was in action again on 7 October during a massive strike by the Eighth (more than 1400 bombers, plus 350 from the Fifteenth Air Force up from Italy) against a wide range of oil industry and other targets throughout the Reich. The Luftwaffe threw everything it had at the attackers, including the Me 163 rocket-fighters of I./JG 400 and the Me 262 jets of the *Kommando* Nowotny.

Once again it appears that the two Focke-Wulf *Gruppen* became embroiled with the bombers' supporting fighters. I./JG 2, commanded now by Hauptmann Walter Matoni (he had been transferred across from I./JG 11 at the end of September), was fortunate to escape with just one pilot killed after being bounced by a swarm of Thunderbolts northwest of Bonn. Hauptmann Bruno Stolle's I./JG 11 lost two pilots, but claimed

four P-47s in return. It was shortly after this that I./JG 11 was stood down, joining JG 1 which was still undergoing a protracted period of rest and re-equipment after its mauling in France.

With JGs 2 and 26 continuing to fly in support of the crumbling western front, October brought a further batch of decorations awarded in tardy recognition of earlier Defence of the Reich successes. Two were again posthumous. Hauptmann Hans-Heinrich Koenig, the erstwhile *Gruppenkommandeur* of I./JG 11, had already been honoured with a posthumous Knight's Cross on 2 September. A similar decoration was now to be conferred upon 1./JG 1's Leutnant Anton-Rudolf Piffer on 20 October. And four days later Major Josef Wurmheller, the late *Gruppenkommandeur* of III./JG 2, was awarded the Swords posthumously. Both 'Toni' Piffer and 'Sepp' Wurmheller had been killed over France in mid-June. Still very much alive, although with an eye injury that was temporarily preventing him from adding to his long list of victories, Leutnant Wilhelm Hofmann, the *Staffelkapitän* of 8./JG 26, received the Knight's Cross on 24 October.

It was to be November 1944 before the Eighth Air Force began losing heavy bombers to the Luftwaffe's Focke-Wulfs again, although in nothing like the numbers that had been brought down during the desperate air battles of the spring and early summer. Of the 40 bombers that failed to return from a 1000+ raid on synthetic oil plants and rail targets in central Germany on 2 November, two of them were claimed by III./JG 54.

This *Gruppe* had been transferred from Russia to France in early 1943 as the first stage of what was intended to be the exchange of JGs 26 and 54 between western and eastern fronts. In the event this plan was never carried out to the full, and III./JG 54 was the only *Gruppe* to make the move westwards. It converted from Bf 109s to Fw 190s just before the invasion of Normandy, and suffered heavily in the fighting that followed. In mid-August the unit was withdrawn from the invasion front for further re-equipment, becoming the first *Gruppe* to receive the new Focke-Wulf Fw 190D-9 – the 'Dora' or, more colloquially, the 'Long-nose'.

One of the two Flying Fortresses downed near Osnabrück on 2 November fell to Oberleutnant Hans Dortenmann, *Staffelkapitän* of 12./JG 54. After 14 previous victories in Russia and six on the invasion front, this would be Dortenmann's only heavy bomber success. Typically for this late stage of the war, his remaining 17 kills – with the exception of a single unfortunate AOP machine – would all be Allied fighters, the last a pair of Soviet Yaks.

On 21 November the Eighth's bombers returned yet again to strike

. . . for the latter date was the day of the unsuccessful 20 July plot to assassinate Adolf Hitler, after which Germany's armed forces were forbidden to use the military salute and ordered instead to give the so-called *deutscher Gruss* – more commonly known as the 'Heil Hitler'. The officer demonstrating it here is Oberleutnant Wilhelm Hofmann, the *Staffelkapitän* of 8./JG 26, who is reporting to his *Geschwaderkommodore*, 'Pips' Priller (left). Contrary to some accounts, Hofmann was not another one-eyed Defence of the Reich ace. The eye-patch was the result of an accident suffered on 22 October 1944, which deprived him of the ability to focus his left eye

at the same combination of oil and rail targets within the Reich's borders. And for the first time in nearly six months Focke-Wulfs of JG 1 were scrambled to meet them. Although they claimed five B-17s – one of which provided Leutnant Emil Demuth, the experienced *Staffelkapitän* of 3./JG 1, with the 12th *Viermot* of his long career – the young pilots that made up the bulk of Hauptmann Hans Ehlers' 'rejuvenated' I./JG 1 were no match for the bombers' 600+ escorting Mustangs. The *Gruppe* suffered 15 killed or missing and five wounded, and lost 26 fighters to the P-51s.

Typical for the late war period, Oberleutnant Hans Dortenmann, who led 14./JG 26 (ex-11./JG 54) during February-March 1945, numbered just one heavy bomber success among his final total of 38 kills. He is pictured here climbing out of his Fw 190D-9 'Black 1' at Varrelbusch in mid-March

Another Fw 190 *Gruppe* in action on this date was a relative newcomer to daylight Defence of the Reich operations. III./JG 301 had started life as I./JG 302, one of the single-engined *Wilde Sau* nightfighter units set up in the latter half of 1943. Redesignated to become III./JG 301 in August 1944, it began exchanging its original Bf 109s for Fw 190s the following month. The *Gruppe* claimed just one B-17 on 21 November, the Flying Fortress shot down south of Magdeburg being the 14th heavy bomber in the career of 9./JG 301's Feldwebel Willi Reschke. It was the first credited to him while flying an Fw 190 in Defence of the Reich, however, as the previous 13 – most, if not all of them, machines of the Fifteenth Air Force – had been achieved on Bf 109s mainly over southeast Europe. Reschke would add six more US bombers to his list of kills before war's end, making him one of the only two known *Viermot* aces to emerge during this final phase of the campaign.

Hauptmann Johannes 'Focke' Naumann, *Gruppenkommandeur* of II./JG 6, sports the Knight's Cross awarded on 9 November 1944. He would end the war as a major flying the Me 262 jet fighter with JG 7

The other was Oberfeldwebel Josef Keil of 10./JG 301, who opened his score with a brace of B-24s near Hildesheim five days later (Reschke was also being credited with a Liberator during this engagement). A total of 14 Luftwaffe *Jagdgruppen* were scrambled on 26 November to oppose this latest in the Eighth Air Force's long series of 1000-bomber raids on German oil and rail targets. They claimed 32 bombers in all – American losses were actually 34! – with three B-17s going to pilots of JG 1. The defenders were forced to pay an exorbitant price for this success, with 60 pilots being killed, 32 wounded and 123 fighters lost or written off.

Now that the end was drawing nigh, the number of decorations seemed to be on the increase. Among November's awards was a Knight's Cross for Hauptmann Johannes 'Focke' Naumann – currently serving as the *Gruppenkommandeur* of II./JG 6 – conferred on 9 November. Another Knight's Cross went to Leutnant Gerhard Vogt, the *Staffelkapitän* of 5./JG 26, on 25 November. The latter date also saw the Oak Leaves presented to Hauptmann Georg-Peter 'Schorsch' Eder, ex-JGs 2, 1 and 26, who had transitioned to Me 262 jet fighters in the immediate aftermath of the Normandy campaign.

5 December offered another stark reminder of just how low the anti-bomber fortunes of JG 1's two Focke-Wulf *Gruppen* had sunk. They

failed utterly to break through to the Flying Fortress formations *en route* to Berlin, becoming inextricably entangled instead with the strong screening force of escorting P-51s. Although the Fw 190 units submitted claims for 16 Mustangs shot down in 25 minutes of violent, individual dogfighting, it had cost them 20 pilots killed or missing, 12 wounded and the loss of a further 38 of their fighters. The destruction of a single B-17 close to the Dutch border during the bombers' return flight by Major Karl Borris, the long-serving *Gruppenkommandeur* of I./JG 26, was poor recompense (the Americans did, however, admit to the loss of 12 of their bombers in total).

Eleven days later, on 16 December, Hitler unexpectedly launched his massive counter-offensive along a 45-mile stretch of the Ardennes front from Malmédy, in Belgium, down to Echternach, in Luxembourg. Almost the whole of the Luftwaffe's fighter strength in the west, with the exception of JG 301, was temporarily relieved of its Defence of the Reich duties and ordered instead to provide direct tactical support for the troops fighting on the ground in the Ardennes.

The timing of the 'Battle of the Bulge', as it has since become commonly known, was heavily dependent upon the weather. Bad weather was vital to the success of the operation, and for a whole week the adverse conditions kept most of the Allied air units based in the UK and northwest Europe firmly on the ground as predicted by the German meteorologists. When, on the morning of 23 December, the early mist and ground fog lifted to reveal a clear blue sky, enemy air power immediately reasserted itself. Hundreds of Allied aircraft dominated the battlefield, forcing the Luftwaffe's *Jagdgruppen* to fight what was, in effect, a second Normandy.

During the first seven days of the 'Bulge' JGs 1 and 11 had, between them, suffered just four Fw 190 combat fatalities in isolated dogfights. However, on 23 December the Allies flew an estimated 5000 sorties, including more than 600 by medium bombers. The Focke-Wulfs of I./JG 11 encountered some of the latter when they intercepted a force of about 60 unescorted Martin B-26 Marauders near Koblenz. In a running fight back towards Belgium that lasted less than ten minutes, they brought down 18 of the US medium bombers. This was one of the last notable successes to be achieved by Focke-Wulfs in German airspace, although strictly speaking it was not in defence of the Reich and it certainly had not been against heavy bombers. The day had cost Hauptmann Rüdiger Kirchmayr's *Gruppe* seven of its own pilots killed or missing, three wounded and a total of 17 Fw 190s lost or written off.

There was one *Gruppe* that *had* been in action against four-engined bombers on this 23 December. The pilots of II./JG 26 were flying their first mission in their new Fw 190D-9 'Long-noses' when they intercepted a daylight force of RAF Lancasters targeting railway yards at Cologne. They were credited with the destruction of six of the British bombers. *Gruppenkommandeur* Major 'Toni' Hackl claimed the first (whose pilot, 110-mission veteran Sqn Ldr Robert Palmer of No 109 Sqn, would be awarded a posthumous Victoria Cross), while two of the other five fell to Oberleutnant 'Waldi' Radener, the *Kapitän* of 7. *Staffel*.

The following day, 24 December, the Eighth Air Force launched the largest air strike of the entire war when it despatched more than

One of the last Fw 190 Defence of the Reich anti-bomber aces of the war, Feldwebel Willi Reschke of 9./JG 301 got his fifth – a B-24 over Hannover – on 24 December 1944. He is shown here as an oberfeldwebel wearing the Knight's Cross received on 20 April 1945, by which time he was flying Focke-Wulf Ta 152s with the *Geschwaderstab* JG 301

2000 heavy bombers against 20+ Luftwaffe airfields and communications targets in western Germany. Just 12 failed to return! JG 1 managed to down a single Flying Fortress, which provided Hauptmann Hermann Staiger, *Kommandeur* of II. *Gruppe*, with his second Fw 190 heavy bomber kill. Staiger was, in fact, one of the leading *Viermot* aces of the Defence of the Reich campaign, but his previous victories had all been scored either on Bf 109s or during operations over France.

Only two of 24 December's dozen bomber losses were B-24s. Feldwebel Willi Reschke of 9./JG 301 was credited with a pair of Liberators destroyed over Hannover on this date, the second of which took his Fw 190 heavy bomber tally to five.

The Eighth lost four more B-24s on 25 December, but overclaiming was still prevalent on both sides and I./JG 1 alone was credited with bringing down seven Liberators! Among the *Gruppe's* claimants were *Kommandeur* Hauptmann Hans Ehlers and Leutnant Emil Demuth, the *Staffelkapitän* of 3./JG 1. They were to be the final bomber victories of the campaign for the two pilots – their 20th and 13th respectively. Demuth would go on to add two last fighters to his score before sharing in the trials and tribulations of JG 1's conversion to the radical Heinkel He 162 *Volksjäger* jet fighter in March 1945. Hans Ehlers, however, was one of the ten pilots who failed to return from a ground-support mission flown by 18 of I./JG 1's Focke-Wulfs in the Bastogne area on the morning of 27 December. The *Gruppenkommandeur's* 'White 20' was shot down by Mustangs close to the Belgian border.

In all, the Focke-Wulf *Gruppen* involved in supporting the Ardennes counter-offensive lost nearly 150 pilots killed, missing or captured, plus many more wounded. And for those fortunate enough to have survived to the end of the year, worse was about to come.

Operation *Bodenplatte*, the Luftwaffe's ill-judged and ill-fated attack on Allied airfields in France and the Low Countries on New Year's Day 1945, is too well known to warrant detailed description here. Suffice it to say that – on this one day alone – the dozen Fw 190 *Jagdgruppen* involved lost a total of 144 fighters between them, with the vast majority of their pilots being either killed or captured.

There were many well-known names participating in *Bodenplatte*. Leading JG 3's attack on the airfield at Eindhoven, in Holland, was its *Geschwaderkommodore*, Major Heinz 'Pritzl' Bär, who was reportedly piloting an Fw 190D-9. And still in attendance was the faithful Oberfeldwebel Leo Schuhmacher, flying as a member of the *Stabsschwarm*. Bär claimed two Typhoons that were just taking off from the target field, but Schuhmacher's machine (an Fw 190A-9) was badly damaged by anti-aircraft fire. He was forced to belly-land the fighter before reaching base, sustaining slight injuries in the process.

Fate was far less kind to the highest scoring surviving *Experte* of the Defence of the Reich campaign. JG 11's veteran NCO Alwin Doppler, now promoted to leutnant and serving as the *Kapitän* of 2. *Staffel*, was shot down during the *Geschwader's* attack on Asch, a newly constructed airstrip located just within Belgium's border with Holland. Doppler's Focke-Wulf crashed little more than five miles from the objective and he was buried close to where he fell. However, due to a mix-up in the records, a further 50 years would pass before his remains were properly identified.

Another *Viermot* ace, Walter Köhne, who had been credited with 15 heavy bombers while flying as an NCO with I./JG 1, but who had also since been commissioned and was now a leutnant and *Staffelkapitän* of Bf 109-equipped 6./JG 11, claimed what is believed to be his final kill of the war when he brought down a P-47 during the attack on Asch.

In the midst of the mayhem that was *Bodenplatte*, the fact that the Eighth mounted a series of strikes against oil installations and numerous road and rail targets in western and central Germany later on the morning of 1 January 1945 is often overlooked. Elements of JG 301 were scrambled from their base at Stendal, some 60 miles to the west of Berlin, upon the reported approach of several small formations of Flying Fortresses. While the *Geschwader's* high-altitude Fw 190D-9s kept the bombers' surprisingly weak escort occupied, the Fw 190As headed for the 'heavies'.

One fell to 10. *Staffel's* Oberfeldwebel Josef Keil almost immediately. Another was sent down in the same area near to Gardelegen by Feldwebel Willi Reschke of 9./JG 301, but the latter pilot ventured too close to his burning victim. Hit by return fire, he was forced to bail out. The Flying Fortress was to be Reschke's seventh and last Fw 190 Defence of the Reich heavy bomber. Shortly after its despatch, 'Jupp' Keil was credited with sending another B-17 down close to Stendal.

On 2 January Hauptmann Walter Matoni was awarded the Knight's Cross. He had claimed ten Defence of the Reich *Viermots* while a member of JG 26, but had been severely injured in a take-off accident on 6 December 1944 little more than two months after being appointed *Gruppenkommandeur* of I./JG 2.

There was to be one last major air battle in the Defence of the Reich campaign when, on 14 January 1945 – two weeks after *Bodenplatte* – no

Fw 190D-9 'Long-noses' of 3./JG 26 taxi out from the cover of the trees at a snow-covered Fürstenau in the winter of 1944-45

5./JG 26's Oberleutnant Gerhard Vogt, an ace with six heavy bombers to his credit, was shot down in his Fw 190D-9 'White 13' by P-51 Mustangs near Cologne on 14 January 1945

Fw 190D-9s of 7./JG 26 emerge from hiding and taxi along a woodland perimeter track towards the runway at Nordhorn-Clausheide in February 1945

fewer than 25 Luftwaffe *Jagdgruppen* were sent up to oppose yet another massive strike by the Eighth Air Force against oil targets and road and rail bridges in central and western Germany. The fact that the defending fighters were unable to claim a single one of the nearly 900 bombers parading across the skies of the Reich was proof, if further proof were needed, of the Americans' now absolute air superiority.

And even the Luftwaffe's claims for two-dozen enemy fighters destroyed on this date pales into insignificance when compared with their own catastrophic losses – 107(!) pilots killed or missing, 32 wounded and close on 150 aircraft lost or written off. The two ex-*Wilde Sau Geschwader*, JGs 300 and 301, which had not taken part in *Bodenplatte*, suffered most. Their seven *Gruppen* alone accounted for almost precisely half of all the casualties with 54 killed and 15 wounded. Included among the day's dead were five *Staffelkapitäne*. One of them was Oberleutnant Gerhard Vogt of 5./JG 26. The Defence of the Reich Fw 190 heavy bomber ace fell victim to a surprise attack by P-51 Mustangs to the southeast of Cologne before he could get anywhere near the Flying Fortress formations heading for the city's Rhine bridges.

The widespread aerial engagements – 'massacre' might not be too strong a word – of 14 January marked the virtual end of Defence of the Reich operations. Hitler now clearly regarded the advancing Red Army as the greater threat to Germany. In a replay of the previous summer's events, which saw the wholesale transfer of the *Luftflotte Reich's Jagdgruppen* westwards in response to the Allied invasion of Normandy, so now the homeland was once again stripped of its fighter defences (or what was left of them) as nearly every unit was rushed eastwards. Just four days after the bloodbath of 14 January, JG 1 was reporting the loss of its first Focke-Wulfs to Soviet Yak fighters.

Almost certainly the last pilot to join the ranks of the Fw 190 Defence of the Reich *Viermot* aces was Oberfeldwebel Josef 'Jupp' Keil of 10./JG 301. The B-17 that he shot down near Berlin on 20 February was the fifth and final heavy bomber of his operational career. Keil's Flying Fortress had been part of Operation *Clarion*, officially described as 'a major assault on German road and rail communications by Allied air forces'. To the attackers, *Clarion* might have been a metaphorical call to arms, but for the Reich's few remaining defenders, the missions flown on that 20 February had more the sound of a death-knell.

Still wearing the patch to protect his injured left eye, Oberleutnant Wilhelm Hofmann, now the *Staffelkapitän* of 5./JG 26, is seen here in the cockpit of his Fw 190D-9. He would be shot down in error by his wingman north of Rheine on 26 March 1945 – the last Fw 190 Defence of the Reich heavy bomber ace to be killed in the war

The rest of the story is quickly told. On 12 March Oberleutnant Waldemar 'Waldi' Radener, long-serving member of JG 26, but latterly the *Gruppenkommandeur* of II./JG 300, was awarded the Knight's Cross. That same month also witnessed the loss of the last Fw 190 Defence of the Reich ace to be killed in action. Oberleutnant Wilhelm Hofmann, the *Staffelkapitän* of 5./JG 26, was leading a small formation of the *Geschwader's* Fw 190D-9s on an anti-*Jabo* (fighter-bomber) sweep near Münster on 26 March when, despite the poor visibility, he managed to claim an RAF Tempest. Hofmann did not return from the mission,

The end of the Defence of the Reich road. The campaign left Germany's cities, industries and airfields in ruins. It also left the remains of many of the Focke-Wulfs that had fought and lost the campaign scattered across the face of the Reich. For example, 11./JG 26's 'Yellow 8' was an Fw 190D-9 found abandoned at Fassberg, near Hannover, with its propeller blades hacked off . . .

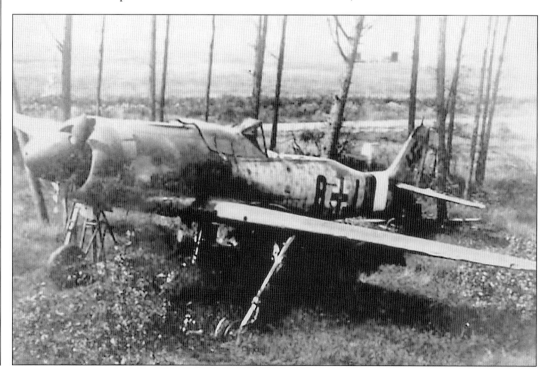

. . . 'Yellow 17' of I./JG 301 was captured almost intact by US forces at Pilsen, in Czechoslovakia . . .

. . . and the carcass of 2./JG 11's 'Black 10' was still lying on the apron at Darmstadt in 1946

and nobody witnessed his demise. It later transpired, however, that he had fallen victim to the inexperience of his own wingman – the youngster had shot him down in error.

Two further Knight's Crosses followed in April. Both went to successful Defence of the Reich NCOs Oberfeldwebeln Erwin Laskowski of 8./JG 11 and Willi Reschke, now of the *Geschwaderstab* JG 301. And exactly 18 days after the latter's award, the war – and with it the last flickering embers of the hard-fought Defence of the Reich campaign – came to an end.

APPENDICES

APPENDIX 1

REPRESENTATIVE ORDERS OF BATTLE

Fw 190 UNITS IN DEFENCE OF THE REICH[1]

A: May 1943 – *Luftwaffenbefehlshaber Mitte*

Unit	CO	Base	Est-Serv
Stab JG 1	Obstlt Hans Phillip	Jever	3 - 1
I./JG 1	Hptm Emil-Rudolf Schnoor	Arnhem-Deelen	31 - 27
II./JG 1	Hptm Dietrich Wickop	Woensdrecht	39 - 31
Stab JG 11	Maj Anton Mader	Husum	4 - 2
I./JG 11	Maj Walter Spies	Husum	40 - 27

Luftflotte 3

Unit	CO	Base	Est-Serv
Stab JG 2	Obstlt Walter Oesau	Beaumont-le-Roger	4 - 4
I./JG 2	Maj Erich Hohagen	Beaumont-le-Roger	40 - 36
II./JG 2	Hptm Erich Rudorffer	(Normandy)	24 - 18
III./JG 2	Hptm Herbert Huppertz	Vannes	40 - 37
Stab JG 26	Maj Josef Priller	Lille-Vendeville	4 - 4
II./JG 26	Hptm Wilhelm-Ferdinand Galland	Vitry-en-Artois	40 - 35

Totals			**269 - 222**

B: May 1944

Luftflotte Reich[2]

Unit	CO	Base	Est-Serv
Stab JG 1	Obst Walter Oesau	Bad Lippspringe	2 - 2
I./JG 1	Hptm Hans Ehlers	Bad Lippspringe	43 - 15
II./JG 1	Maj Heinz Bär	Störmede	42 - 20
I./JG 11	Oblt Hans-Heinrich Koenig	Rotenburg	28 - 20
III./JG 11	Maj Anton Hackl	Oldenburg	28 - 11
III./JG 54	Hptm Werner Schroer	Landau	23 - 8
Stab JG 300	Maj Kurt Kettner	Merzhausen	2 - 1

Luftflotte 3

Unit	CO	Base	Est-Serv
Stab JG 2	Obstlt Kurt Bühligen	Creil	3 - 0
I./JG 2	Maj Erich Hohagen	Aix	19 - 14
III./JG 2	Hptm Herbert Huppertz	Creil	29 - 19
Stab JG 26	Obstlt Josef Priller	Lille-Nord	2 - 2

| I./JG 26 | Hptm Karl Borris | Lille-Vendeville | 33 - 23 |
| II./JG 26 | Hptm Johannes Naumann | Cambrai-Süd | 32 - 25 |

| **Totals** | | | **286 - 160** |

C: January 1945

Luftflotte Reich

Stab JG 300	Maj Kurd Peters	Jüterbog	6 - 4
Stab JG 301[3]	Maj Fritz Auffhammer	Welzow	5 - 5
I./JG 301?	-	Finsterwalde	38 - 26
II./JG 301[3]	Hptm Herbert Nölter	Welzow	40 - 38
III./JG 301	Maj Guth	Alteno	26 - 20

Luftwaffenkommando West [4]

Stab JG 1	Obstlt Herbert Ihlefeld	Twente	5 - 4
I./JG 1	Oblt Emil Demuth	Twente	27 - 22
II./JG 1	Oblt Fritz Wegner	Drope	40 - 30
Stab JG 2[3]	Obstlt Kurt Bühligen	Nidda	4 - 3
I./JG 2[3]	Hptm Fritz Karsch	Merzhausen	28 - 23
III./JG 2[3]	Hptm Siegfried Lemke	Altenstadt	19 - 6
Stab JG 6	Obstlt Johann Kogler	Quakenbrück	4 - 3
I./JG 6	Hptm Ewald Trost	Delmenhorst	34 - 27
II./JG 6	Hptm Johannes Naumann	Quakenbrück	48 - 39
Stab JG 11	Maj Jürgen Harder	Biblis	7 - 6
I./JG 11	Hptm Rüdiger Kirchmayr	Darmstadt	23 - 20
III./JG 11	Oblt Paul-Heinrich Dähne	Gross-Ostheim	42 - 26
Stab JG 26[3]	Obst Josef Priller	Fürstenau	3 - 3
I./JG 26[3]	Maj Karl Borris	Fürstenau	60 - 36
II./JG 26[3]	Maj Anton Hackl	Nordhorn	64 - 42
III./JG 26	Hpt Walter Krupinski	Plantlünne	56 - 28
III./JG 54[3]	Oblt Hans Dortenmann	Fürstenau	47 - 31
IV./JG 54	Hptm Rudolf Klemm	Vörden	50 - 39

| **Totals** | | | **676 - 481** |

D: April 1945

Luftflotte Reich

Stab JG 2[3]	Obstlt Kurt Bühligen	Eger	5 - 3
II./JG 2[3]	Hptm Fritz Karch	Karlsbad	8 - 4
III./JG 2[3]	Hptm Siegfried Lemke	-	12 - 9
Stab JG 4[3]	Obstlt Gerhard Michalski	Mark Zwuschen	6 - 4
Stab JG 26[3]	Maj Franz Götz	Uetersen	4 - 3
I./JG 26[3]	Maj Karl Borris	Sülte	44 - 16
II./JG 26[3]	Hptm Paul Schauder	Uetersen	57 - 29
Stab JG 301[5]	Maj Fritz Auffhammer	Neustadt-Glewe	3 - 2
I./JG 301[3]	Hptm Posselmann	Hagenow	35 - 24
II./JG 301[3]	Maj Roderich Cescotti	Neustadt-Glewe	32 - 15

Luftflotte 6

Stab JG[3][3]	Maj Werner Schroer	-	4 - 4
Stab JG 6[3]	Maj Gerhard Barkhorn	(Niederlausitz)	4 - 4
II./JG 6[3]	Hptm Müller	(Niederlausitz)	48 - 45
Stab JG 11[3]	Maj Anton Hackl	Strausberg	4 - 4
I./JG 11	Hptm Karl Leonhard	Strausberg	55 - 53
III./JG 11[3]	Hptm Herbert Kutscha	Strausberg	54 - 51

Totals	**375 - 270**

Key

1 - Does not include Fw 190 Sturmgruppen
2 - Redesignated from Luftwaffenbefehlshaber Mitte on 3/2/44
3 - Wholly or partially equipped with Fw 190D-9
4 - Redesignated from Luftflotte 3 on 28/9/44
5 - Equipped with Focke-Wulf Ta 152

APPENDIX 2

Known Fw 190 Defence of the Reich anti-bomber Aces*

Name	JG(s)	Defence of the Reich Heavy Bomber Victories	Total Number Heavy Bomber Victories	Final Score	Fate
Piffer, Ltn Anton-Rudolf	1	26	26	35	17/6/44 kia
Doppler, Ltn Alwin	11	25	25	29	1/1/45 kia
Hermichen, Maj Rolf	26, 11	20	20	64	s
Ehlers, Maj Hans	1	20	20	52	27/12/44 kia
Koenig, Oblt Hans-Heinrich	11	19	20	28	24/5/44 kia
Schnoor, Maj Emil-Rudolf	1	18	18	23	16/4/44 ifa
Bär, Maj Heinz	1	17	19+	220	s
Engleder, Hptm Rudolf	1	17	19	20	s
Hübl, Ofw Rudolf	1	16	17	20	27/6/44 kia

Hackl, Maj Anton	11, 26	15+	32	192	s
Radener, Oblt Waldemar	26	15	19	36	s
Köhne, Ofhr Walter	1	15	15	30	s
Stöwer, FhjOfw Heinz	11	15	15	16	30/5/44 kia
Koch, Hptm Harry	1	13	13	30	22/12/43 kia
Demuth, Ltn Erich	1	13	13	17	s
Clausen, Hptm Erwin	11	12	12	132	4/10/43 mia
Grislawski, Hptm Alfred	1	11	17	132	s
Kirchmayr, Hptm Rüdiger	1	11	11	29	s
Bach, Lt Otto	1	11	11	12	26/11/44 kia
Matoni, Maj Walter	26, 1	10+	14	44	s
Eder, Oblt Georg-Peter	1	10	35+	78	s
Glunz, Oblt Adolf	26	10	19	71	s
Huppertz, Hptm Josef	2	10	17	78	8/6/44 kia
Willius, Lt Karl	26	10	12	50	8/4/44 kia
Schrangl, Oblt Hans	11	10	10	13	s
Steiner, Fw Franz	11	10	10	12	s
Pancritius, Oblt Hans	11	10	10	10	17/7/43 kia
Mayer, ObstIt Egon	2	9	26	102	2/3/44 kia
Zick, Ofw Siegfried	11	9	17	31	18/7/44 wia
Oesau, Oberst Walter	1	9	10	118	11/5/44 kia
Laun, Ofw Hans	1	9	9	11	30/7/44 kia
Schueking, Fw Norbert	11	9	9	11	s
Reschke, Fw Willi	301	7	20	27	s
Laskowski, Ofw Erwin	11	7	10+	35	s
Schuhmacher, Ltn Leo	1	7	10+	23	s
Segatz, Hptm Hermann	1	7	7	40	8/3/44 kia
Fuchs, Fw Heinz	1	7	7	11	24/2/44 kia
Frey, Hptm Hugo	11	6	26	32	6/3/44 kia
Vogt, Oblt Gerhard	26	6	8	48	14/1/45 kia
Naumann, Hptm Johannes	26	6	7	34	s
Scheyda, Ofhr Erich	26	6	7	29	7/5/44 kia
Zwernemann, Oblt Josef	11	6	6	126	8/4/44 kia
Hoeckner, Hptm Walter	1	6	6	68	25/8/44 kia
Lüth, Ofw Detlef	1	6	6	38	6/3/44 kia
Wurmheller, Hptm Josef	2	5	21	102	22/6/44 kia
Hondt, Lt Erich	11	5	7+	15+	s
Hofmann, Oblt Wilhelm	26	5	6	44	26/3/45 kia
Rathenow, Fw Johannes	1	5	6	7	3/11/43 kia
Keil, Ofw Josef	301	5	5	10	s
Güthenke, Lt Hans-Georg	11	5	5	7	12/5/44 wia
Dreizehner, Ofhr Gerhard	11	5	5	6	9/4/44 kia

* This list makes no claim to be complete, let alone definitive. In some instances it is difficult to establish exactly which of a pilot's heavy bomber victories were scored while flying the Fw 190, or claimed during the course of a Defence of the Reich sortie. This is particularly so in the case of JG 2 (Kurt Bühligen and Fritz Karch – credited with 24 and 21 heavy bombers respectively – are obvious omissions). The list is therefore offered primarily as a guide for further research.

Key
kia - killed in action
mia - missing in action
wia - wounded in action
ifa - injured in flying accident
s - survived the war

COLOUR PLATES

1

Fw 190A-7 'White 20' of Major Emil-Rudolf Schnoor,
***Gruppenkommandeur* I./JG 1, Bad Lippspringe, April 1944**

The long-serving Schnoor is believed to have been one of the first unit commanders to use numerals (usually in the 20-26 range) in place of the geometric *Stab* symbols as laid down in regulations for the identification of HQ machines. The reason for this change is not certain, although it may have been intended to render them less conspicuous to enemy fighters in the air. In addition to the *Geschwader* badge on the engine cowling and JG 1's red Defence of the Reich aft fuselage band, 'White 20' also sports Schnoor's personal marking below the windscreen – an intertwined 'Double M', which has a ribald connection with the pilot's home city of Hamburg.

2

Fw 190A-8 'White 20' of Hauptmann Hans Ehlers,
***Gruppenkommandeur* I./JG 1, Greifswald, November 1944**

Depicted at Greifswald on the Baltic coast towards the end of JG 1's lengthy post-Normandy period of rest and re-equipment, Ehlers' A-8 does not yet display the red aft fuselage band that would be applied before the unit re-entered the Defence of the Reich fray during the latter half of November 1944. Ehlers, who had replaced Schnoor at the head of I./JG 1 after the latter's serious accident back in mid-April (and who had retained the 'White 20' *Gruppenkommandeur's* marking), was shot down by P-51s west of Koblenz on 27 December.

3

Fw 190A-5 'White 7' of Unteroffizier Walter Köhne, 1./JG 1, Arnhem-Deelen, July 1943

In the early months of the campaign prior to the introduction of Defence of the Reich coloured aft fuselage bands, Köhne's 'White 7' carried no identifying unit makings, but it was adorned with a girl's name ('Uschi' – a diminutive of Ursula) below the cockpit. The all-white engine cowling was designed to facilitate the unit's regrouping in the air for a second pass after the initial coordinated attack on a bomber formation. It is believed, however, that due to confusion arising from the white forward cowling rings worn by the Americans' first P-47 escort fighters, JG 1 subsequently added black horizontal stripes to its white cowlings.

4

Fw 190A-6 'White 5' of Unteroffizier Rudolf Hübl, 1./JG 1, Arnhem-Deelen, December 1943

By late 1943 I./JG 1's cowlings had undergone further change, and some were now displaying an elaborate black-and-white checkerboard pattern. This marking also had unfortunate repercussions. One day in the spring of 1944, or so the story goes, the *Gruppe's* base at Deelen was strafed by P-47s from the USAAF's 78th FG, which were sporting newly introduced black-and-white checkerboard markings. The airfield's flak gunners held their fire, believing the 'attackers' to be their own fighters intent on a friendly beat-up, instead of which – in the words of one witness – the field was given 'a thorough going-over'. Not surprisingly, the fancy paint jobs on the cowlings of the *Gruppe's* machines disappeared almost overnight! Note the small device painted below the cockpit. This is believed to be Hübl's personal emblem – the face of 'Grock', a famous Swiss clown who was hugely popular with German circus audiences in the 1930s.

5

Fw 190A-8 'White 3' of Leutnant Anton-Rudolf Piffer,
***Staffelkapitän* 1./JG 1, Le Mans, June 1944**

In contrast to the increasingly striking markings carried by I./JG 1's machines during the early months of the Defence of the Reich campaign, the Fw 190A-8s that Hauptmann Ehlers' *Gruppe* took to the Normandy invasion front were plain to the point of anonymity. 'White 3', the fighter in which leading Fw 190 anti-bomber *Experte* 'Toni' Piffer was killed in a clash with Mustangs west of Argentan on 17 June, displays no embellishments other than yellow cowling undersides and a spiralled spinner.

6

Fw 190A-6 'Black 3' of Oberleutnant Rudolf Engleder, 2./JG 1, Arnhem-Deelen, September 1943

A brief return to the more colourful markings of early autumn 1943 with Rudolf Engleder's 'Black 3', which displays an 'interim' black-and-white horizontally striped cowling. By the beginning of 1944 most 2. *Staffel* machines would also be wearing red Defence of the Reich aft fuselage bands and the *Geschwader's* 'Winged 1' badge newly introduced by *Kommodore* Oberstleutnant Walter Oesau. This badge was carried on the *left* side of the cowling only.

7

Fw 190A-8 'Yellow 7' of Oberfähnrich Walter Köhne, 3./JG 1, Bad Lippspringe, May 1944

Walter Köhne's A-8 is depicted here in pre-Normandy livery. The fancy cowling paintwork has disappeared, leaving just the *Geschwader's* identifying red aft fuselage band. Now that the erstwhile unteroffizier (corporal) has been elevated to oberfähnrich (officer aspirant) and transferred to 3. *Staffel*, it would appear that the unfortunate Uschi – see profile 3 – is no longer the object of his affections. Her name has gone the way of the decorated cowlings, to be replaced below the cockpit sill by the much more enigmatic *'Löwe'* ('Lion').

8

Fw 190A-7 'Red 22' of Oberfeldwebel Leo Schuhmacher,
***Gruppenstab* II./JG 1, Störmede, April 1944**

II./JG 1 also dispensed with their geometrical *Gruppenstab* markings sometime in late 1943 or early 1944 – probably the latter, for when Major Heinz Bär assumed command of the *Gruppe* in mid-March 1944, it is known that he had his aircraft marked as 'Red 13'. This was Bär's lucky number. He had scored his first kill as a feldwebel in 'White 13' (a Bf 109E of JG 51) back in September 1939 and, circumstances permitting, remained superstitiously true to this same numeral throughout the war. The members of his *Stabsschwarm* at Störmede in the spring of 1944 flew machines numbered in the low 20s, with 'Red 22' being the mount of his then regular wingman Oberfeldwebel Leo Schuhmacher.

9

Fw 190A-5 'Yellow 12' of Oberleutnant Harry Koch, *Staffelkapitän* 6./JG 1, Woensdrecht, April 1943

II./JG 1 had originally been formed in January 1942 by simply redesignating I./JG 3, a *Jagdgruppe* recently returned from the eastern front. This unit's emblem was the *'Tatzelwurm'*, a mythical creature – half-dragon/half-worm – that had adorned the cowlings of its Bf 109s since the days of the *Blitzkrieg* in France. It survived the unit's redesignation and its subsequent conversion to the Fw 190. The *'Tatzelwurm'* was always painted in the relevant *Staffel* colour, hence the yellow example seen here on the machine flown by Harry Koch, the recently appointed *Kapitän* of 6./JG 1.

10

Fw 190A-4 'Yellow 8' of Oberfeldwebel Leo Schuhmacher, 6./JG 1, Rheine, July 1943

Leo Schuhmacher had begun his career as a *Zerstörer* pilot, claiming his first victories against the RAF over the North Sea in 1940. After a lengthy spell as an instructor, he joined II./JG 1 in the winter of 1942-43, being assigned to 6. *Staffel.* The latter was commanded at that time by Harry Koch's predecessor, Oberleutnant Walter Leonhardt. An early casualty of the Defence of the Reich campaign, Leonhardt had been killed in action against Flying Fortresses on 4 February 1943 during only the second incursion into German airspace by bombers of the Eighth Air Force.

11

Fw 190A-7 'Yellow 7' of Major Heinz Bär, 6./JG 1, Rheine, January 1944

Wearing the Oak Leaves with Swords, and with almost 200 aerial victories to his name, Major Heinz Bär was a surprising addition to the ranks of 6./JG 1 late in 1943. Although officially the 'deputy Staffel leader', this posting was without doubt a disciplinary measure against the high-ranking Bär and was possibly the nadir of his mercurial operational career. Stripped of his previous authority, he was unable to fly an Fw 190A carrying his preferred lucky number '13', but had to be content at first with the 'Yellow 7' depicted here (not for long, however – see caption to profile 8).

12

Fw 190A-4 'Yellow 12' of Unteroffizier Hans-Georg Güthenke, 9./JG 1, Husum, March 1943

Back almost a year to the time immediately prior to the division of the original JG 1 to form JG 11, Güthenke's 'Yellow 12' wears standard camouflage and markings of the period, plus JG 1's early 'Maltese cross' *Geschwader* shield below the cockpit and 9. *Staffel's* badge on the rear fuselage. The latter, showing an antique flintlock pistol superimposed on a red heart, bore the inscription *'Wer zuerst schiesst hat mehr vom Leben'* ('He who shoots first gets more from life' – in other words, 'lives longest').

13

Fw 190A-4 'White Chevron and Triangle' of Hauptmann Egon Mayer, *Gruppenkommandeur* III./JG 2, Cherbourg-Théville, February 1943

Egon Mayer's A-4 displays a wealth of markings. Reading from the left, the 'Cockerel's head' *Gruppe* badge introduced by his immediate predecessor, Major Hans 'Assi' Hahn, the stylised black panel surrounding the engine exhaust louvres, a *Kommandeur's* white geometric 'Chevron and triangle' symbol and, behind the fuselage *Balkenkreuz*, the thin band – also white outlined in black – which III./JG 2 used to identify its *Gruppenstab* machines. Like many of JGs 2 and 26's *Experten*, Mayer kept a detailed record of his victories on the rudder of his aircraft. His tally here opens with a single French fighter, which is followed by 51 RAF machines. The six double bars marked with a star are his first half-dozen USAAF heavy bombers (all downed over France during the winter of 1942-43). After another quartet of RAF fighters and eight more Flying Fortresses, again all claimed over France, Egon Mayer would be credited with his first Defence of the Reich victim on 30 July 1943.

14

Fw 190A-5 'Yellow 2' of Oberleutnant Josef Wurmheller, *Staffelkapitän* 9./JG 2, Vannes, May 1943

'Sepp' Wurmheller's 'Yellow 2' also displays an immaculately kept rudder scoreboard. The 60 victories that earned him the Oak Leaves on 13 November 1942 are encompassed by the decoration at the top. Next comes a row of nine RAF kills, followed by two American, one RAF and two more American. The latter represent his first four US heavy bombers (separated by a single RAF Typhoon) brought down over France. He was to add another 11 Flying Fortresses (and four Spitfires) in the west before claiming his first Defence of the Reich heavy bomber on 8 February 1944. The latter would not be claimed in this particular 'Yellow 2', however, as it was written off in a ground accident at Vannes on 29 July 1943 and replaced by an identically marked A-6.

15

Fw 190A-7 'Black Chevron and Triangle' of Hauptmann Rolf Hermichen, *Gruppenkommandeur* I./JG 11, Rotenburg, March 1944

By early 1944 the markings of I./JG 1 and I./JG 11 could hardly have been more different. While the former *Gruppe*, stationed in Holland, had been experimenting with their striking cowling designs, I./JG 11, based at Rotenburg to the east of Bremen, had all but obliterated their machines' national insignia. The real reason for this has never been fully explained, but it may perhaps have been for camouflage purposes in the often-murky weather conditions prevailing over northern Germany at this time – an early form of today's low-visibility markings, in fact. Hermichen's aircraft, already wearing an exceptionally pale finish, provides a prime example. The only clue to its parent unit is the Defence of the Reich aft fuselage band in yellow, the colour assigned to JG 11.

16

Fw 190A-7 'Black Chevron and Vertical Bar' of Leutnant Hans Schrangl, *Gruppen-Adjutant* I./JG 11, Rotenburg, March 1944

This Fw 190A-7, flown by Hermichen's *Gruppen*-Adjutant Hans Schrangl, has likewise had its fuselage *Balkenkreuz* and tail swastika completely oversprayed, but its more standard camouflage scheme lends it an altogether less 'spectral' appearance (note, however, that both machines retain their underwing crosses).

17

Fw 190A-7 'Black Chevron and Triangle' of Oberleutnant Hans-Heinrich Koenig, *Gruppenkommandeur* I./JG 11, Rotenburg, May 1944

Another obvious difference between I./JG 1 and I./JG 11 is that the latter's *Gruppenstab* Focke-Wulfs all displayed regulation geometric symbols. After Rolf Hermichen's posting to a staff appointment in May 1944, his place at the head of I./JG 11 was taken by Oberleutnant Hans-Heinrich Koenig, hitherto the *Kapitän* of 3. *Staffel*. 'King' Koenig initially retained the aircraft he had flown with 3./JG 11 – hence the clear signs of the overpainting of a previous numeral behind the freshly applied *Kommandeur's* chevron and triangle. Note also the 27 victory bars displayed on the rudder.

18

Fw 190A-7 'Black 10' of Oberfeldwebel Alwin Doppler, 2./JG 11, Rotenburg, March 1944

This anonymous A-7 is one of the mounts of Alwin Doppler, possibly the most successful of all the Fw 190 Defence of the Reich anti-bomber aces. Some sources have suggested that his *Viermot* total was in fact 33, and not the 25 as listed in Appendix 2. If just two of his eight unconfirmed claims actually *were* kills, it would place him above the accepted leading Fw 190 *Experte*, Leutnant Anton-Rudolf Piffer of 1./JG 1. Although Doppler was recommended for the Knight's Cross in May 1944, it had still not been awarded at the time of his loss – by which point he was both a leutnant and the *Kapitän* of 2. *Staffel* – during Operation *Bodenplatte* on 1 January 1945.

19

Fw 190A-5 'Yellow 12' of Oberleutnant Hans Pancritius, *Staffelkapitän* 3./JG 11, Dörpen, June 1943

A reconstruction of the A-5 flown by 'Pankraz' Pancritius, the first Fw 190 pilot to bring down five US heavy bombers during the course of Defence of the Reich operations. He is unique in that *all ten* of his final tally of victories were US four-engined bombers (eight B-17s and two B-24s). Pancritius would be lost in action over the North Sea on 17 July 1943 while trying to claim his 11th.

20

Fw 190A-6 'Yellow 7' of Fahnenjunker-Feldwebel Hans-Georg Güthenke, 3./JG 11, Husum, August 1943

The rudder tally on Hans-Georg Güthenke's 'Yellow 7' dates this profile to the latter half of 1943. There was very nearly a seven-month gap between his third victory indicated here, a Flying Fortress downed on 28 July 1943, and the next – another B-17 – on 21 February 1944. Note the narrow white band aft of the fuselage *Balkenkreuz* (thought to be an air-to-air recognition device used by 3./JG 11 at this time), and also the fact that the *Staffel* badge has now been moved from the position on the rear fuselage that it occupied during the unit's days as 9./JG 1 (see profile 12) to the engine cowling.

21

Fw 190A-6 'Yellow 10' of Feldwebel Heinz Stöwer, 3./JG 11, Husum, September 1943

This is the machine of another Defence of the Reich anti-bomber *Experte* in the making, the first of the two victory bars seen on the rudder here being for the Beaufort shot down by

Heinz Stöwer during the RAF Coastal Command attack on the German cruiser *Prinz Eugen* off the southwest coast of Norway on 17 May 1942. The second, claimed exactly 15 months later, was for a Flying Fortress – possibly *'Our Gang'* of the American 91st BG – downed *en route* to Schweinfurt on 17 August 1943. Stöwer would be credited with 15 US 'heavies' in all before himself falling victim to P-51s on 30 May 1944 during the Eighth's final raid on Germany prior to D-Day.

22

Fw 190A-7 'Yellow 12' of Leutnant Hans-Georg Güthenke, 3./JG 11, Rotenburg, May 1944

The last Fw 190 flown in combat by Hans-Georg Güthenke (see profiles 12 and 20), this was the machine in which he was badly injured when he collided with his fifth and final heavy bomber victim northeast of Prum on 12 May 1944 – the first day of the Eighth's offensive against the German oil industry. Although 'Yellow 12' has had its national insignia overpainted, it still retains 3. *Staffel's* badge on the cowling.

23

Fw 190A-7 'White 7' of Oberfeldwebel Siegfried Zick, 7./JG 11, Oldenburg, March 1944

Depicted shortly after III./JG 11's conversion from Bf 109Gs to Fw 190As in January 1944, 'White 7' clearly shows that this *Gruppe* also chose (or was ordered?) to overspray its machines' fuselage *Balkenkreuze* and tail swastikas. The only basic difference between the aircraft shown here and those of I./JG 11 seen earlier in the colour section is the vertical III. *Gruppe* bar superimposed on the yellow Defence of the Reich band. Siegfried Zick's 17 heavy bomber victories were almost equally divided between the two types of fighters he flew, as he got his first eight on Messerschmitts, followed by nine on Focke-Wulfs.

24

Fw 190A-6 'Black Chevron and Horizontal Bars' of Oberstleutnant Josef Priller, *Geschwaderkommodore* JG 26, St Omer-Wizernes, February 1944

Strictly speaking, Josef Priller is not an Fw 190 Defence of the Reich anti-bomber 'ace' in the accepted *Osprey* meaning of the word. However, although only three of his 11 heavy bomber claims are thought to have involved machines engaged against targets inside Germany's borders, he is such an iconic figure in the Luftwaffe's fight against the Eighth Air Force's daylight bombing offensive that the inclusion of one of his aircraft is not out of place here. Like 'Pritzl' Bär, 'Pips' Priller was greatly attached to the lucky number '13' and always flew machines carrying this numeral during the later stages of his career. This particular A-7 is therefore something of an oddity. The textbook set of pre-war regulation *Kommodore's* markings may, however, have been applied solely for the occasion of Generalfeldmarschall Erwin Rommel's visit of inspection to the Geschwader, which was officially filmed for the weekly news-reels. For shortly after Rommel disappeared, so too did the chevron – to be replaced by the number '13'!

25

Fw 190A-4 'Black Double Chevron' of Hauptmann Wilhelm-Ferdinand Galland, *Gruppenkommandeur* II./JG 26, Volkel, August 1943

'Wutz' Galland, a younger brother of *General der Jagdflieger* Adolf Galland, was another of JG 26's leading *Experten* who just failed to make it to heavy bomber acedom in Defence of the Reich. Exactly half of his eight bomber victories were scored against enemy formations flying missions aimed at targets within Germany. The last was a Flying Fortress claimed near Bonn on 12 August 1943, five days before he himself was brought down by P-47s during the closing stages of 'First Schweinfurt'. Note that this A-4 – like that of Egon Mayer's depicted in profile 13 – features an external supercharger air intake scoop on each side of the engine cowling for improved high-altitude performance.

26
Fw 190A-7 'White 5' of Oberleutnant Walter Matoni, *Staffelkapitän* 5./JG 26, Cambrai-Süd, March 1944

One member of JG 26 who *was* an Fw 190 Defence of the Reich anti-bomber ace – possibly even the most successful of all – was Oberleutnant Walter Matoni. Ten of the 11 heavy bombers he claimed while with the *Geschwader* had been engaged in operations against Germany. After six months service as the *Staffelkapitän* of 5./JG 26, the then Hauptmann – later Major – Matoni was appointed *Gruppenkommandeur*, in turn, of I./JG 11, I./JG 2 and, finally, II./JG 2. The full details of the last three of his overall total of 14 heavy bombers are unfortunately not known.

27
Fw 190A-6 'Yellow 1' of Hauptmann Hans Naumann, *Staffelkapitän* 6./JG 26, Vitry-en-Artois, July 1943

This rather plain Fw 190A-6, devoid of any unit or personal decorations, is the mount of Hans 'Focke' Naumann, depicted towards the end of his 11-month stint as the *Staffelkapitän* of 6./JG 26. By this time (late July 1943) his score – which he had opened with an RAF Spitfire shot down over the Thames Estuary at the height of the Battle of Britain – had risen to 18, and already included the first two of the six Flying Fortresses that he would duly claim during 6./JG 26's Defence of the Reich operations.

28
Fw 190A-8 'Black 9' of Leutnant Adolf Glunz, *Staffelkapitän* 6./JG 26, Guyancourt, June 1944

Kapitän of the new 6. *Staffel* (redesignated from 5./JG 26 in October 1943), 'Addi' Glunz was another of JG 26's foremost *Experten*. The rudder scoreboard tells the story. At the top, his first 30 victories are indicated within the ribbon of the Knight's Cross, which he had received on 29 August 1943. The 32 black kill bars below, although bearing no details, include all ten of his confirmed Defence of the Reich heavy bomber successes. This machine replaced the earlier Fw 190A-7 that Glunz had flown whilst serving as *Kapitän* of 5. *Staffel*, and which is seen in a photograph on page 63.

29
Fw 190A-8 'Brown 13' of Leutnant Gerhard Vogt, *Staffelkapitän* 7./JG 26, Guyancourt, June 1944

The 28 victories recorded on the rudder of Vogt's Fw 190A-8 date this to the latter half of June 1944. They include all six of his recent Defence of the Reich heavy bomber successes, the first downed during the 8 March raid on Berlin and the last

claimed during a later American strike against the same target on 29 April. Gerhard Vogt was another pilot with an apparent – but unfortunate – predilection for the number '13'. He wrote off this particular machine in a forced landing on 5 July 1944 after tangling with RAF Spitfires southeast of Argentan. And he would lose his life at the controls of Fw 190D-9 'White 13' on 14 January 1945 when bounced by P-51 Mustangs near Cologne (see the specially commissioned cover art of this volume for Mark Postlethwaite's dramatic depiction of this latter incident).

30
Fw 190A-7 'Blue 14' of Leutnant Wilhelm Hofmann, *Staffelkapitän* 8./JG 26, Cambrai-Süd, April 1944

Depicted as flown in mid-April 1944, Hofmann's 'Blue 14' displays 12 victory bars on what appears to be a replacement (or overpainted?) rudder. Among the 12 are his five Defence of the Reich heavy bombers – three B-17s and a pair of B-24s – all claimed between January and April 1944. After very nearly a year as *Staffelkapitän* of 8./JG 26, Hofmann took over at the head of 5. *Staffel* in February 1945, only to be shot down in error by his eager, but inexperienced young wingman the following month.

31
Fw 190A-8 'Black Chevron and Horizontal Bars' of Major Anton Hackl, *Geschwaderkommodore* JG 76, Freiburg, September 1944

One of the Luftwaffe's true *Experten*, 'Toni' Hackl's varied and highly successful operational career spanned the entire six years of the war. Rising from unteroffizier to oberleutnant with JG 77, he was subsequently posted to JG 11, being appointed *Kommandeur* of III./JG 11 in October 1943. It was after this *Gruppe's* conversion from Messerschmitts to Focke-Wulfs in January 1944 that he scored the majority of his 15+ Fw 190 Defence of the Reich heavy bomber victories. In August 1944 'Toni' Hackl assumed command of the short-lived JG 76 (flying the Fw 190A-8 depicted here), before taking over II./JG 26 in October. He then commanded JG 300 during January-February 1945, before returning to JG 11 – this time as the unit's *Geschwaderkommodore* – late in February. Hackl was still with the unit at war's end.

32
Ta 152H 'Green 9' of Oberfeldwebel Willi Reschke, *Geschwaderstab* JG 301, Neustadt-Glewe, April 1945

Willi Reschke's first 13 bomber successes had been scored mainly over southern Germany and Hungary during the high summer of 1944 while flying Bf 109s with 1./JG 302. He then added seven more – all within the Reich – after the *Staffel's* redesignation as 9./JG 301 and its conversion to Fw 190s. His last, a B-17, went down over Gardelegen on 1 January 1945. Two months after that Reschke was transferred to the *Geschwaderstab* of JG 301, which was equipped with the Ta 152, the last operational fighter from Kurt Tank's wartime design stable. There are no known heavy bomber victories attributed to Ta 152 pilots, but in the closing weeks of the war Willi Reschke was able to claim no fewer than three Allied fighters – an RNZAF Tempest V south of Schwerin on 14 April 1945 and a pair of Soviet Yak-9s over central Berlin two days later.

INDEX

References to illustrations are shown in **bold**. Plates are shown with page and caption locators in brackets.